discover your spiritual type

A GUIDE TO INDIVIDUAL AND CONGREGATIONAL GROWTH

corinne ware

THE
ALBAN
INSTITUTE

Library of Congress Catalog Card Number 95-75681
ISBN 1-56699-149-8

For Jenny, Max, and Caleb

*Written in the hope that this book will make yours
a more inclusive world.*

Occasionally, a single word appears at the confluence of great intellectual currents. A word that seems to belong in each, yet combine all. In this generation, "consciousness" is such a word.

Lawrence Kushner
The River of Light, 1981

There are many ways toward the vision, but the vision itself is one and exercises a control over the plurality of spiritual disciplines.

John Macquarrie
Principles of Christian Theology, 1977

CONTENTS

FOREWORD

When Celia Hahn, our editor in chief at The Alban Institute, asked me to write a foreword to this book, I groaned. Where would I find time to read another book and write a foreword? "You're going to love it and use it a lot," she said, "so you might as well read it now and write a foreword for us."

She was right. I did love it. And I intend to use it a lot.

For starters, *The Spirituality Wheel* immediately helped me understand why fundamentalists and charismatics have a hard time with each other; why Jerry Falwell had trouble gaining credibility with the PTL Club.

It also helped me understand why Shalem Institute for Spiritual Formation here in Washington, D.C., has carved out such a niche for itself within the spiritual landscape of this country. For the past fifteen years the Shalem Institute has offered courses in contemplative spirituality and has been training people to offer spiritual direction. It has reached a clientele that is not being served well by mainline congregations.

The Spirituality Wheel also gave me a fix on why books on spirituality and the "soul" are selling like hot cakes, while all mainline denominations are experiencing a decline in membership. Thomas Moore has become a celebrity with his publications of *Care of the Soul* and *Soul Mates*. Other books that have hit it big are Betty J. Eadie's *Embraced by the Light* (the tale of a Midwestern mother's near-death experience), Dannion Brinkley's *Saved by the Light* (another hot-selling testament of life after death), and James Redfield's novel *The Celestine Prophecy* (the story of a spiritual quest in Peru that's racked up a million and a half in hardcover sales). Even the music biz is getting into the soul game. The gargantuan success of *Chant*—a double-platinum collection of Gregorian chants sung by the reclusive Benedictine Monks of Santo Domingo de Silos—has led to spin-offs, including *Chant Noel.*

Why this phenomenon of best-selling religious material while millions of Protestant and Catholic congregations are struggling to stay alive? This book gives explanations that make sense. It can give congregational leaders a better fix on their clientele and the kind of adult classes, seminars, or retreats that might have some appeal to those who have spiritual hungers the church is not meeting.

More important, this book and its test instrument when offered to an entire congregation can identify where the members score in terms of spiritual typology; it can help certain members identify how and why some of their spiritual needs are not being met by congregational life. This instrument gives the congregation an opportunity to structure classes and retreats that would more fully meet the spiritual needs of those members. In the process some of those same activities might attract newcomers.

Another distinct use of the Spirituality Wheel could be during a congregational search for a new pastor. I see value in having a search committee ask its hottest prospects to read the book and take the inventory. In an interview the candidate and the committee could explore together the spiritual typologies in the book and discuss what kind of match they think they would make given the congregation's predominate type and the candidate's.

I personally intend to use the Spirituality Wheel in some of my seminars with clergy. Seminaries offered so little on spirituality and most clergy, I believe, would respond well to the insights offered in this book. Together we could explore what type of spirituality most appealed to each participant, and then place the indicated typology alongside that of the participant's congregation. This would give clergy a better handle on tension points in their relationships with the congregations or with certain people within their congregations.

I anticipate that seminar participants will have the same "aha" experience that I had when I took the survey and read the book. I am a type 4 on the Spirituality Wheel with some strong affinity to type 3. The congregation to which I belong fosters a strong type-1 spirituality, yet there is enough openness in the congregation for me and my wife, Carole, to offer adult seminars that grow out of our spiritual typology.

This past Christmas, on our ten hour drive back from relatives in

Canada, Carole and I had a very insightful conversation as we explored the various types on the Spirituality Wheel. For years now we have not been able to agree on the type of ministry we eventually wish to conduct on the eighty acres of mountain land we own in the Cacoctin Mountains here in Maryland. Carole advocated this being a place of retreat for people needing solitude and healing away from the noise and pollution of the city. I have leaned more toward this being a place where the poor and disenfranchised could find a way of starting over again to gain a new lease on life. It was no surprise to us to discover that she is a type 3 (contemplative) on the Spirituality Wheel while I am a type 4 (crusader). Acknowledging our differences on the Spirituality Wheel has taken us a whole lot closer to resolving our differences with regard to our vision.

As you can see, I've made immediate practical use out of this instrument and this book. You have done yourself a real favor in buying the material. Corinne Ware has done all of us a favor in taking the concepts originally identified by Urban T. Holmes and reworking these into truly usable and helpful material. I predict the spiritual types developed in this book will become as common to our vocabulary as are the types laid out in the Myers-Briggs Type Indicator.

Roy Oswald
December 29, 1994

The purpose of this book is to enlarge the reader's consciousness of God, of others who worship God, and of oneself. Specifically, it asks why some people worship one particular way, while others choose a very different way of expressing religious devotion. Why do we feel as we do about worship and our God-connection, often yearning for something we cannot describe? Finally, this book is about types of spirituality.

My interest in the subject rises out of my personal experience and that of others whom I serve as a pastoral counselor. Those who are dissatisfied with their faith experience make a common complaint: that they do not seem to "fit" in their worship group. These are often deeply religious people and their distress is genuine. In my work I began to see that many of the problems did not have to do with development and maturity. Much of the distress comes out of a deep inner sense that natural tendencies are either being violated by present worship patterns or simply not being allowed expression by those practices.

There are several ways of determining maturity of religious experience, but few people have addressed spirituality *type*. Characteristics of religious faith have been commented on by Freud, Jung, Fromm, James, Frankel, and recently by Fowler in his 'stages of faith' construct. The typology presented in this book may appear to be part of that genre, but is not. The approach used here *delineates differences*; it does not rank experience in terms of maturity.

Several years ago I came across the spirituality typology of Urban T. Holmes and realized that it provided a conceptual framework that could be used to determine type. I decided to try and find ways to adapt Holmes's ideas and make a testing instrument that would answer my questions about spirituality type. The test I developed is included here, along with a description of how to use its results.

This book is intended for two kinds of readers. One is the individual on a spiritual journey who wants to explore and grow in that "walk." Some of these people will be engaged in the discipline we call "spiritual direction," that ancient and, until fairly recently, forgotten skill practiced by one who is called to accompany others in their spiritual journey. (The word *direction* is one I would not choose, but I use it here because of its familiarity.) I hope that the insights provided in this book will help the individual reader understand his or her personal spirituality and foster and deepen inner experience. I also hope spiritual directors find this a useful tool to help them better interpret the needs of those with whom they work.

The second audience is the reader interested in providing growth experiences within the spiritual life of a worshipping congregation. The testing instrument used is called the Spirituality Wheel Selector test. It has no right or wrong answers, just preferences. It can provide a spiritual portrait of your group, telling you where your corporate strengths lie and pointing to areas of most productive growth. Because this book will be used as a study guide for workshops, here is a chapter by chapter summary.

Chapter 1 poses the questions that can be answered when the spirituality typology test is taken and analyzed by individual people and by congregational groups. The chapter closes with an introduction to the spirituality typology.

Chapter 2 lays the foundation for the study of types by discussing the terms *integration* and *individuation* as psychological components of spiritual wholeness. The person of Jesus is presented as a model for spiritual wholeness.

Chapter 3 is the heart of the book in that it delineates the four spirituality types, describing each.

Chapter 4 includes the Spirituality Wheel Selector. The reader has permission to photocopy the test.

Chapters 5 and 6 are designed for congregational and group use. Chapter 5 outlines workshop formats, giving easy-to-follow instructions for conducting one-day, one-week, and two–week studies. Chapter 6 discusses ways of using congregational feedback gained from the test.

Chapter 7 is for the individual on a personal spiritual journey or in spiritual direction with others.

Chapter 8 details an experiential exercise called *lectio divina*, which uses all four types of spiritual expression to study a single passage of scripture. You will find that it is a particularly effective way to meditate and to prepare a lesson or sermon.

Chapter 9 is a discussion of how Holmes links periods of history to the type of spiritual expression it fosters. It is a fascinating hypothesis that can lead to lively discussion.

Chapter 10 closes the study with some thoughts on how the reader can internalize and carry out some of the things learned about spiritual type.

The appendix gives an extra copy of the basic Spirituality Wheel Selector test, as well as slightly altered versions for Roman Catholic and Jewish readers. The three tests are essentially the same but differ slightly in vocabulary, reflecting the worship practices of particular groups. For those planning a congregational workshop, an order form for additional books is found at the end.

Spirituality, it seems, has suddenly become "religiously correct." This is regrettable insofar as it can trivialize our deepest feelings. It is also cause for hope if, because of the current interest, we discover more about our own spiritual lives. I hope your pleasure in thinking about these ideas of spiritual type is as great as mine has been in presenting them.

ACKNOWLEDGMENTS

Many people have contributed to the development of this study. It began as a project dissertation for a doctor of ministry in pastoral counseling degree and continues as a growing body of work now being used by individual people and by congregations. As all of us know, we are indebted to people from our past who made "invisible investments," the value of which we cannot begin to calculate. To those who offered encouragement, made scholarships available, found books, taught classes, and arranged all manner of things not always part of their job descriptions, I owe many, many thanks.

My special thanks to Prof. John H. Westerhoff III, for copies of class materials used in his course on spirituality at the Divinity School, Duke University, Durham, North Carolina. Thanks also for his telephone calls and letters that helped me to focus on significant features found in the typology developed by his friend and colleague Urban T. Holmes. Although he cannot be held responsible for the conclusions presented here, Dr. Westerhoff has been very instrumental in their development.

Another source of academic help came from Prof. W. Paul Jones, Saint Paul School of Theology, Kansas City, Missouri. I am grateful for his clarifying comments on comparisons between the spiritual types of Holmes and the psychological types of Jung as seen in the Myers-Briggs Type Indicator, a subject in which he is expert.

I express gratitude to all librarians everywhere whose payment can never equal the service they provide. Particular thanks to Thomas Edward Camp, Librarian, School of Theology, The University of the South, Sewanee, Tennessee, for assembling for me valuable biographical material on Urban T. Holmes.

Prof. Wade Rowatt was my faculty adviser at the Southern Baptist

Theological Seminary, Louisville, Kentucky. He encouraged and guided my efforts to do a project dissertation in spirituality for the doctor of ministry in pastoral counseling degree. Gary Augustin, Ph.D., director of the Samaritan Center where I do my pastoral counseling work as a clinical therapist, also served as an important mentor for the project.

I gratefully acknowledge the important contribution of my long-time friend Don Strickland of Austin, Texas, who with great patience taught me to use a Macintosh computer. Graduate academic study and writing for publication would be impossible, it seems to me, without that important skill. A new friend is Celia Allison Hahn, Editor in Chief for The Alban Institute. Her confidence in this work and her gentle guidance to its completion brought the project to print. Many thanks to Evelyn Bence who took a somewhat wordy manuscript and made it clearer.

To those who participated in testing the Spirituality Wheel Selector test as well as other less effective instruments, I give great thanks. They helped refine and correct the final outcome. The Clinical Pastoral Education group of 1992 at Heartland Health System, under the direction of Rev. Sally Schwab, was especially helpful in providing ideas about testing and what works in group settings. Gratitude also to those clients in individual spiritual direction with me at Samaritan Counseling Center; they provided insight into how the spirituality typology works when used with individual people.

Finally, I extend warm thanks to Jane Neighbors Holmes, wife of Urban T. Holmes and executrix of his estate, for her kind permission to use the materials found in the introduction to his book *A History of Christian Spirituality*. She has been gracious in letting me share his important insights into the varieties of spiritual types.

CHAPTER I

Are There Really Types of Spirituality?

Have you ever been in a worship service where you felt you did not "fit"? Those around you were nice enough; they appeared to be sincere, but something was lacking; you left feeling your spiritual needs had not been met.

Perhaps you are very satisfied with your worshipping community—their religious expression. But you may be puzzled that others seem less content than you; they agitate for change in ways you find disruptive. Why do they seem so out of joint with what you find spiritually nourishing?

Or you may be a worship leader, a program planner, or a member of a staff search committee. Why is it that some in the congregation are satisfied, even enthusiastic, about the style of worship and the congregational activities, while others range from apathetic to downright hostile? Leaders want to understand their memberships to better meet the needs of the worshipping group. They raise questions: What is our church really like compared to other churches? What do we most need to strengthen our congregation and meet the needs of more of the people we serve? What would we have to do to relieve some of the discontent?

These questions can essentially be reduced to two: "Who am I as a spiritual person?" and "What is the spiritual profile of my worshipping group?" If you were able to answer these questions, what difference would it make to you? Knowing how you are spiritually different from or the same as other people can help you understand where your strengths are and possibly acknowledge the strengths of others. Such knowledge may suggest new ways in which you and your congregation can grow so that spiritual experience becomes richer and stays on the growing edge.

Marie is a sixty-seven-year-old woman who is married with two grown children. She comes to the pastoral counseling center where I work, seeking individual spiritual direction. She has never used a counseling service before and is visibly uneasy about the prospect. Yet her anxiety over her inner questions is great enough to make her risk the unfamiliar. In our first interview, she blurts out painfully, "I must not be 'spiritual'!" She goes on to describe her local church worship experience; her friends find their religious life quite satisfying—but not she. She feels herself to be a deeply religious person. But if that is true, how is it that she feels so empty after a worship service? After exploring what is going on within her, we agree that indeed she is a profoundly "spiritual" person, but her personal spirituality is not of the same type she finds in her church. Marie comes to understand that this is neither good nor bad; it is simply different. Although I have changed her name, Marie's story is true and representative of many others.

Acknowledging that there are differences in the way people feel about and respond to patterns of worship implies that there are types of spirituality. Most of us are horrified to think that someone might attempt to "measure" spiritual life. How can anyone know how spiritual a person or a group is? And if someone could know such a thing, is it the business of anyone but the individual and God? At the outset, we need to say that spiritual depth cannot be accurately measured and that it is not the purpose of this study to try.

We are not interested in "how much spirituality?" but in "what *kind* of spirituality?" Just as we learned from the temperament types proposed by Carl Jung[1] (and tested by Isabel Myers and Katherine Briggs,[2] and by David Kiersey and Marilyn Bates[3]), so we are able to learn from the study of *spiritual types* proposed by Urban T. Holmes, whose work is foundational for this book.

Being able to identify the spiritual style of your worshipping group and knowing your personal style of spirituality will help you see how you fit within the group; it may suggest ways to care for unmet spiritual needs. Understanding spiritual types can also provide insight to church planners trying to identify strengths and opportunities within the church.

The Spirituality Wheel: Questions It Asks and Answers

It is important to our study that we look at both corporate and individual needs.

Congregational Questions

The spiritual types presented here can address a number of questions asked by church leaders and planners. These questions about corporate spirituality include:

How do our members see this church? If you were to survey congregational members, how would they describe what they experience when they attend your worship service? Do they say they leave having had something valuable to *think* about during the week? Or would they be inclined to say that they had experienced a deep *emotional* connection with God? Both are high values, but they are *different* values.

What is the spirituality type of the majority of our members? If you were able to evaluate the type of spiritual needs that characterized each individual, what different types of needs would you discover in your congregation? What percent favors an intellectual approach to faith, and what percent prefers the more affective or emotional experience of inner warmth? Some may be "doers" who contend that faith without "feet" is useless. A few may be yearning for a Christian version of the mystic experiences they read about in New Age spiritualities. A worship experience cannot meet all the needs of each worshipper, and indeed it should not try, but knowing what kind of worshipper you are addressing helps as a guide to meeting the needs of most.

How can we provide enriched experiences for those whose needs are not being met? In chapter 7 we will discuss ways by which the needs of each type can be met legitimately. At this point, it is important to consider the idea that there are many ways to worship, not just one *right way*. Although it is true that different denominational and established religious groups are characterized by "type," just as people are different in type, each group has some latitude within its own structure. A group must remain faithful to its mission and basic belief system. That does not imply, however, that the individual spiritual needs of its members are irrelevant. Ministry, after all, is about people and not about structure. A primary purpose of religion is to enable connection between the person and the Creator, not simply to protect the institution.

What is our church doing 'right'? If people are coming to worship and you see them growing in their faith, work, and relationships, then something good is going on. To what, exactly, are they responding? What is encouraging this growth? If you know what works, you will know how to support it.

In what ways does our church differ from other types of spiritual expression? This is a question of endless fascination for most of us: Why do they do it that way and we do it this way? One focus of this book and the typology presented here is the appreciation of differences as being essential to what we have come to call *wholeness* in spiritual experience. The ideas we will consider here are not presented in an effort to divide and polarize, so if you tend to be defensive or exclusive, you might not like this way of seeing things.

Individual Questions

In this book we can expect to answer a number of questions asked by individual people who are on a personal quest. Questions include the following:

Do I (and does everyone) have a spiritual self? I've told you the story of Marie, who was afraid she was not "spiritual." She was deeply disturbed by this thought, wondering if some people have a spiritual nature while others do not. Many people not active in church life will tell you that they are not religious, or that they are not very spiritual. Being active in projects and attending worship services is generally equated with spirituality. Thinking about it, however, we know that some of the most peaceful and spiritually sensitive people we know are not all that active as churchgoers. Conversely, there are active church people who are flourishing, while other busy "doers" are anxious, unhappy, and driven. *All* have a spiritual self and are in some way seeking to fill the needs of that part of themselves.

What is my own personal style of spirituality? And what good would it do me if I knew? If you think of it in terms of strengths and of "the growing edge," you can see the value of knowing this about yourself. Many of us have experienced what we would call a spiritually intense moment, perhaps several such moments. Most would agree that it is God who gives the experience and that we are more responsive in some conditions and atmospheres than in others. Certain sights, thoughts, sounds, and contexts make us unusually sensitive to the Holy. And when we become aware of some movement within ourselves that signals the need to grow, we may want to return to those spiritually fertile places. Or we may feel compelled to explore areas that are not so familiar, walking into the "different" or the "other." Knowing our spiritual type will help to guide us in our quest for connecting to the Holy.

How well does the style of my congregation fit with my personal style? Many of us fear that if we dig and discover that our worship and congregational life does not satisfy our spiritual hungers, we will be faced with an intolerable dilemma. Will we have to change churches or synagogues or leave formal religion altogether? Some feeling themselves in damaging situations have done just that in order to be true to their deepest inner voice. Others have dropped out, losing their appetites for spiritual growth. But there is another alternative: understanding what it is we need and meeting that need as well as possible without giving up what has been nourishing in the past. It may require some minor—perhaps major—changes. I can take my time and I can seek guidance, but it does me no good not to understand who I am spiritually.

What is the best way for me to develop my spiritual life? When we feel the agitations that signal change, we often flounder for a while and then stumble onto something that fits. There may be value in this. Knowing what we don't need seems as important as knowing what helps. From the early Church Fathers through the medieval mystics to modern spiritual writers, advice is plentiful on how to advance in the spiritual life. Since this advice differs, it is enormously helpful to find our personal style of growing and the ways in which we most clearly hear God. If you are the sort of person who "hears in the silence," you can seek silence without apology. If, like Brother Lawrence, you learn and grow when your hands are busy serving another's need, then you can cultivate the active moments and experience *being* through the sacrament of *doing*. If you are most moved toward God in the presence of music, you can furnish yourself a rich musical opportunity for worship. If your spirit is stirred by vivid language and new thoughts, you can expose yourself to great writers and to those who convey truth through the spoken word.

Why is my expression of spirituality different from that of others? If you and I are different, I come to know myself by knowing you and through the clarification of contrast. We can come to understand that each of us is unique yet a part of the whole. Our different ways of being need not separate; rather, they can fit together into a spectrum of spiritual life that nourishes each one. I need what you do and who you are for my own fullness, and you need me.

Making a Portrait of My Congregation and of Me

The Spirituality Wheel is a way of drawing a picture of your spiritual identity and the spiritual identity of your worshipping community. It asks you to select one or more statements among several and to see what these choices reveal about your spiritual type. As you use the wheel, a portrait of your spirituality will take shape.

Chapter 4 includes the selector test and instructions for taking it. Since it is not the forced-choice-type test that most of us are used to taking, it needs some explanation; read the directions carefully. There will be two "wheels" presented: one to reflect the kind of worship you experience in your congregation, the other to show your personal preferences and inclinations. From the selector test you can easily compare the two wheels. If you want to know information only about a congregation or only about personal spiritual type, you simply use one of the wheels, not both.

You might apply the test results in several ways. Congregations or smaller groups can evaluate the composition of the group as a whole—what kind of spiritualities the group contains and the implied consequent corporate needs. It will also shed light on what kind of leadership is needed to cause the group to stretch, developing into new areas while conserving the group's strengths.

Individually, you can use the test to "measure" your fit to your congregational worship experience. You may choose to add activities to your spiritual life or subtract them if simplicity and reflection are what you need. In chapter 8 we will explore several ways to nourish your spiritual life and provide the environment that promotes growth for the unique person you are. Knowing your type and needs will enable you to choose what works for you.

Using Holmes's Spirituality Types

This book is about a particular way of seeing ourselves spiritually—about naming the way we are. I will be using the spirituality typology of Urban T. Holmes because I believe it provides a contemporary model that works in today's spiritual climate. It provides a tool and a method by which to conceptualize and name spiritual experience within a basic framework. It is particularly useful in that it helps one position one's own religious experience within the context of the experience of others.

From 1973 until his death in 1981, Holmes was dean of the School of Theology at The University of the South in Sewanee, Tennessee. He wrote numerous articles and books and was a historian of theological ideas. In the introduction to his book *A History of Christian Spirituality* he introduces his typology of spirituality.[4]

Holmes called his construct the "Circle of Sensibility," and in it he delineated four schools of spirituality. Here is an adaptation of his circle.

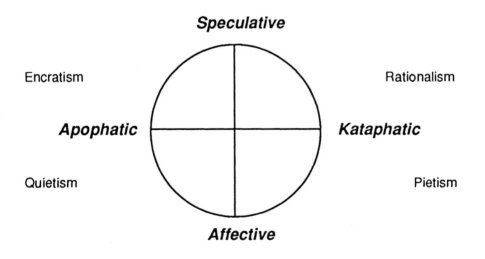

Figure 1: The Circle of Sensibility

Adapted from *A History of Christian Spirituality* by Urban Holmes, III, p. 4, Copyright © 1980 by Urban Holmes, III. Reprinted by permission of Jane Holmes, Executrix.

Holmes defined the word *sensibility* as

> that sensitivity to the ambiguity of styles of prayer and the possibilities
> for a creative dialogue within the person and within the community as
> it seeks to understand the experience of God and its meaning for our
> world.[5]

Holmes proposed the use of two intersecting lines placed within a circle.
His line-scales are identified by descriptive terms long available to
theologians and observers of human nature. It is in combining and
configuring these particular descriptions that he makes a unique contribution to ideas of spiritual type.

The terms chosen by Holmes for his Circle of Sensibility are probably the best to use as far as accurate definitions are concerned. Regret-
tably, the identifying words are unfamiliar, not often used by many
readers. The following circle is identified with more accessible words I
have chosen. Use whichever version makes the most sense to you.

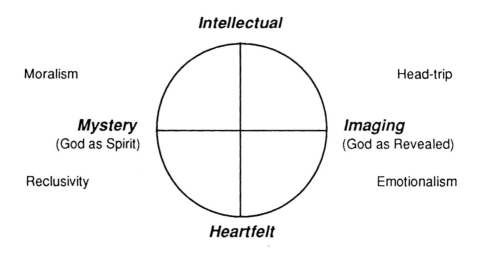

Figure 2: The Circle of Sensibility (terms adapted)

The circle emphasizes Holmes's belief that each of four types of authentic religious experience is needed as part of a healthy whole. The circle itself represents the value placed on unity and on the interdependence of each part. Contained within the circle are the elements that Holmes believes make for wholeness and healthy spirituality; these are the words printed at the four points: the north, south, east, and west terminals. Awareness of the importance and contribution of all four elements in his circle is what Holmes calls "sensibility." That's where he gets his name for his concept, the Circle of Sensibility. We should become sensitive, he says, to the ambiguity of styles in prayer and worship, and to the creative dialogue this promotes within the person and within the community.

Notice that within the circle the lines intersect forming separate quadrants. The quadrants identify four types of spirituality; these will be the basis for the testing done by the Spirituality Wheel.

Notice also the smaller words printed around the circle, between the intersecting axes. We will deal with the meaning of these in chapter 3. For now we can see that they are aberrations of spirituality, excesses peculiar to a particular type. Holmes believed that, carried to excess and without the corrective tension of the other parts, people in any of the four types could fall outside the safety of the circle. Each quadrant has its own aberration, its own extreme, that can damage and restrict growth, both personally and in the community.

Health is found in the "sensibility" of both being aware of the whole and discovering uniqueness and difference. To understand more about this combination of being "one with" and "separate from," we need now to use the vocabulary of psychology: *integration* and *individuation*. Exploring those meanings will lay the foundation for using the test that follows in chapter 4. What would an individual who combined both integration and individuation be like? Let's turn our attention to the person of Jesus of Nazareth and examine what we see there.

CHAPTER II

Integration and Individuation: A Vocabulary for Spirituality

It is important to stop at this point and define some of the terms we are using. Before talking about what encourages one's spirituality to flourish, let us determine what we mean by spirituality itself. The word is often used but rarely defined; it is difficult to pin down its precise meaning. Spirituality often refers to those things that have to do with the intelligent and immaterial part of a person, the part that experiences the transcendent. It also can mean all those attitudes and activities that characterize one's attempts to make connection with Deity. In this study it will be used in this second sense. Holmes speaks of different schools of spirituality, by which he means the various modes of prayer and worship used as a way of connecting. His use of the word will affect our understanding of his ideas about spirituality and spiritual type.

Psychiatrist and writer Scott Peck claims that "everyone has a spiritual life whether they acknowledge it or not."[1] Each of us has a capacity for the "something more," and we sometimes come to points in our lives when we particularly yearn for that something. Saint Augustine's comment made in his *Confessions* is often quoted because it is so true: "Thou hast made us for Thyself, and our heart is restless until it rests in Thee." The restlessness itself tells us that we are spiritual beings.

A Psychological Way of Seeing Wholeness

The terms *integration* and *individuation*, frequently used in the context of psychology, certainly have meaning outside that field. Integration points to one's being embedded in the "given," while individuation points to one's carving out of new territory.

One reason for considering the terms here is because they give foundational meaning to Holmes's circle and its two intersecting axes. Before we study the four spirituality types, in chapter 3, it is important to understand their framework.

The circle motif suggests integration of parts into a whole, while the quadrants or four types formed by the intersecting axes represent individuated parts *of* the whole. This four-part circle is our template for conceptualizing spirituality. A second concept underlies these ideas of circle and parts—that *both* integration and individuation are necessary to a healthy and growing spirituality. They are complementary; two sides of one coin.

Integration

Integration involves bringing together parts into a whole. From the point of view of psychology, one might say, for example, that a manic- depressive patient is disintegrated (disorganized) during the illness and reintegrated (reorganized) following it.[2] Psychologist Abraham Maslow, who has done important work in the area of integration and religious experience, believes that most people think atomistically, that is, in terms of either-or, black-white, and other mutually exclusive categories. This type of thinking is not integrated.

> I see in the history of many organized religions a tendency to develop two extreme wings; the 'mystical' and individual on the one hand, and the legalistic and organizational on the other. The profoundly and authentically religious person integrates these trends easily and automatically.[3]

The person of spiritual integration described here by Maslow is able to participate in forms, rituals, and verbal formulae that remain for him experientially rooted and symbolically meaningful; they are never reduced to the merely behavioral. Such people feel deeply what is said and done in worship; it is not a matter of just going through the motions.

Maslow points out two traps. On one hand, people forget their internal religious experience and redefine religion as a set of habits and dogmas that become legalistic, bureaucratic, conventional, and empty—

that is, *antireligious*. The mystic experience, the illumination or the
"high moment," is lost and churches or synagogues may become the
enemies of the religious experience. There is a tendency in Western
culture to suppress spiritual experience and to deny even the possibility
of the transcendent.

The experiential, or mystic, has its traps as well. Focused on such a
wonderful subjective experience, the mystic may tend to turn away from
involvement with the world, becoming self-absorbed and, finally, utterly
selfish. Religious experience may become addiction, a subject now being addressed by several writers.[4]

Only by holding the tension of outer form with inner meaning can
we arrive at full religious experience.

Healthy spirituality includes not only integration of form with experience, but also integration of past with present. In his treatment of
religious issues that arise in psychotherapy, Robert J. Lovinger points to
the negative memories that may stem from the religion of childhood.[5] If
a child's life was unpleasant or even abusive, the religious associations
of the time can remain arrested, never developing into adult forms and
experience. As the past is discovered and identified, it can be integrated
into the more healthy, creative present; the stunting religious experience
loses its power to contaminate. Personal wholeness includes an understanding and acceptance of one's past. We need not accept that what
happened to us was good, but we must acknowledge that it is *ours*.

One of the chief claims of this chapter is that Jesus is an example of
healthy spiritual life; he integrated form with experience as he combined
past tradition with present reality. We shall examine this claim further
after looking at the second important term, *individuation*.

Individuation

Individuation was a term often used by psychoanalyst Carl Jung. In his
writing he defined it as "the process of forming and specializing the
individual nature . . . a process of differentiation, having for its goal the
development of the individual personality."[6] The word *individuation* has
almost become a dual word, *separation-individuation,* due to the important work of psychiatrist Margaret Mahler. As distinguished by Mahler,
separation refers to the child's movement away from fusion with the

mother, while individuation consists of those steps that lead to the development of an individual's own persona and unique characteristics so that the separation can be endured.[7] Mahler's foundational insights readily translate to religious experience and help us understand some forms of religious anxiety. Individuation is scary! Becoming oneself, independent of others, can be an exciting adventure but it is definitely not a comfortable process.

"There is no more disastrous path than to seek to violate one's basic nature."[8] As Holmes makes clear in his typology, individuation, or developmental progress toward knowing one's own tendencies and gifts, is the way in which we find our own unique spiritual expression. He urges us to "identify our own place within a much wider [religious] tradition."[9] We cannot integrate the potentially enriching experiences of others into our own self-understanding unless we first have a self; to gain a self, we must first relate to and then differentiate from community. It is a continuously enriching circular movement of interaction and definition. Once one is able to accommodate to new configurations of self, the personality remains open to alterations and enrichment. One of the purposes of this study is to encourage and enhance that possibility.

Summary

So it is that one term, *integration*, means effectively fitting together into a whole; the other, *individuation*, describes distinction from the whole. This paradoxical feature is critical to the spirituality typology we are considering here. And it is what we observe in the life of Jesus.

The *Imitatio Christi:* A Feature of Christian Spirituality

Although this book will find its way primarily to readers of the Christian faith, I believe it can be useful to Jewish readers. A valid study of spiritual types should not be limited to one faith group.

There is little dispute about Jesus of Nazareth having been a historical figure. How we regard him is another matter. Our treatment of Jesus here is as an example of developed spirituality seen in a particular person. The Christian reader will think of Jesus by many of the names given to him by the Christian church. The Jewish reader may wish to regard him as Rabbi Yeshua ben Joseph, or by whatever name is in keeping with his or her historical understanding. The effort is not to cloud the issue by claiming a particular faith point of view, a subject that is more than adequately covered by libraries of writings in both Christian and Jewish traditions. Rather, it is to see clearly the way in which one person, common to both strands of history, lived out his faith life. I hope that for the purpose of seeing Jesus as a model of healthy spirituality, this focus on example will be an approach acceptable to the Jewish reader as well as faithful to a Christian understanding of Jesus' identity.

Many readers of this book will be of the Christian faith, and an authentic Christian spirituality is distinguished by the fact that it incorporates and emulates its namesake, the person of Jesus Christ. One of the two or three most widely read religious books, other than the Bible, has been Thomas à Kempis's *The Imitation of Christ*. While some Christians would not agree with parts of Thomas's theology, the book's popularity reflects the general belief that Jesus is an exemplar of the God-connected life. To the Christian he is supreme revelation of how that life is lived. To the Jewish philosopher Martin Buber, Jesus was one who had such a powerful and unconditional relation to his "Thou" that he could say "Father."[10] To Mahatma Gandhi, Jesus spoke the noblest words language is capable of producing. Whatever our view, we can agree that he was an extraordinary person. But why?

Christian spirituality has always had at its heart the *imitatio Christi*, the patterning of one's life after what we know of the life of Jesus. If Jesus' life is illustrative of the ways in which human beings at their fullest spiritual capacity can relate to God, what characteristics can be observed in this example? What makes his a "full" spirituality, if indeed it is that? We will notice two important features that mark the spirituality of Jesus: (1) his embeddedness in and integration of his faith tradition, Judaism, and (2) his individuation into a person of unique spiritual qualities within that tradition. It will be helpful to all readers, Christian or otherwise, to observe behavior of Jesus that shows us what it looks like to live with spiritual integrity.

Jesus' Integration of Spiritual Experience

Evidence for the claim that Jesus integrated his spiritual tradition as well
as his personal history is found in the New Testament gospels. The first
question to be answered is whether Jesus was a cultural anomaly, untouched by his time and place, or was he instead an existential part of
that moment and culture, incorporating his heritage into his self–identity.
Was he somehow untouched by his world, or was it an integral part of
who he was? For answers we look at Jesus' connections to the powerful
Jewish prophetic tradition and to its pervasive wisdom tradition.

The gospels, our only record of Jesus' life, have been critically examined for many years. People are less and less sure about what they
read, and when they ask, "Did this really happen?" or, "Was that really
said?" they voice a certain anxiety. One author sums up the results of
these critical studies by saying that "together with form criticism, redac-
tion criticism has made it even more clear that every story and word of
Jesus has been shaped by the eyes and hands of the early church."[11]

However you may feel about this kind of critical investigation, it is
important to note that a few things have remained intact as verifiable.
One is that Jesus bore the cultural marks and shared much of the world
view of his time and place.[12] He seems to have engaged in the social,
work, and worship patterns typical of his people. He did not explicitly
oppose the law, particularly not laws relating to Sabbath and to food.
His deviations from norms were always within the context of those
norms and were aimed at the restoration, not the destruction, of the community. Contrary to past supposition, the opinion now widely held is
that Jesus subscribed to the Jewish restoration eschatology popular at the
time. His own emphasis while not overtly political was nonetheless that
of restoration. He seems to have thoroughly integrated Jewish tradition
both within his mind and his social expression.

The Prophetic Tradition

At times Jesus seems so embedded in his culture as not to be the inclusive person we expect him to be, based on our impressions of him from
other than gospel accounts. His saying to the Canaanite woman, "I was
sent only to the lost sheep of the house of Israel" (Matt. 15:24), seems

provincial to us now, but it does convey his sense that his mission was activity taking place primarily within Judaism.

Jesus' prophetic consciousness is fruit of his integration of his people's spiritual history. The Jewish prophets were thought to know God in a unique and intimate way.[13] Jesus clearly saw himself to be a bearer of this prophetic legacy. While teaching he remarked, "Prophets are not without honor, except in their home town" (Mark 6:4), and, "It is impossible for a prophet to be killed outside of Jerusalem" (Luke 13:33).

Like the ancient prophets, he experienced a call to vocation. He heard a voice and saw a vision at the time of his baptism by John, a figure compared to Elijah. Mark presents the experience as being private to Jesus in his inner consciousness, while Matthew and Luke report a more public manifestation. The importance of the accounts lies in the hearing of the call by Jesus who interpreted it as the voice of God.

Like Moses and Elijah, Jesus entered the wilderness alone, a classic pattern chosen by those seeking clarification and a deeper connection to the world of Spirit. Here I use the phrase *world of Spirit* or *life of Spirit* to refer to the God-connection that is sought over other alliances. Meister Eckhart helps to explain the yearning for this connection in the desert experience: "The desert is the vast solitude [and] there is no place for two in the desert. The opposition between Creator and creature is abolished."[14]

While in the desert, Jesus prayed, as we shall see him pray throughout his lifetime, in the tradition made available by Judaism: contemplative silence maintained over extended periods of time[15] and meditation focused on particular thought.[16] Verbal expression, such as the Lord's Prayer, is a type more familiar in Western religious practice. The inner life of Spirit is familiar ground and is the more important reality for Jesus. A prophet's willingness to suffer the rejection of his message and the prophet's awareness of the possibility of personal martyrdom are based on the strength of this interior reality.

The unhappy part of Jesus' message, so reminiscent of Jeremiah's warnings, is the admonition to "flee to the mountains" (Luke 21:21), an alarm that seems to be directed at imminent danger rather than toward the end of time. In prophetic tradition the voice of warning is sounded prior to political catastrophe. Like Jesus, the prophets of old were probably more concerned with the dangerous present than with the distant future. Both warned of immediate danger, and both found the message unpopular. Reminiscent of Jeremiah, Jesus cried over his city and the future he intuited. A prophet sometimes predicts the future, but a prophet always addresses him- or herself *to* the future.

The prophetic tradition, and historic Judaism generally, believed in intuition and wisdom-knowledge as being the gift of God. Abraham heard God and saw visions; Jacob stood at the intersection of spirit and matter as he envisioned a ladder; Moses realized he was in Holy Presence at the sight of a bush burning. Whether we see these events as being physical phenomena or interior imagery matters very little. The significance of such accounts is that the participants believed in a world of Spirit and in the possibility of God being present with people. This was a part of their reality.

Jesus is a puzzle to us largely because he belongs to that spiritual world as much as he does to our own more literal, one-dimensional reality. To understand him, we must understand what the reality in his tradition made available. To emulate his pattern of spirituality, we need to engage in an interior life of listening and being attentive to Spirit. Jesus felt God to be both interior and exterior, to be immanent and transcendent, indeed, to be everywhere present. His tradition spoke to him of God in the world (Isaiah 6:3: "the whole earth is full of his glory") and God in the heart (Psalm 51:10: "Create in me a clean heart, O God").

The Wisdom Tradition

"For it is he [God] who gave me unerring knowledge of what exists" (Wisd. of Sol. 7:17). Although people of that time attributed to God the gift of wisdom, Hebrew wisdom literature does not present itself as the product of divine inspiration or lay claim to the status of special divine revelation in the same way that prophetic literature does.[17] The basic form of wisdom expression was the sentence, proverb, or saying—"A short saying based on long experience."[18]

Jesus was neither a writer of what typically falls into the Hebrew wisdom category, nor was he famous for a collection of short, pithy sayings. There are many so-called "sayings" from him, but they do not always have the characteristics of, say, the Proverbs. Jesus' sayings were aphoristic in style—a short-shot of wisdom—and they seem to have been a natural part of his conversation. They include wisdom sayings such as

"Do not worry about tomorrow, for tomorrow will bring worries of its own" (Matt. 6:34) and prophetic statements like "The time is fulfilled, and the kingdom of God has come near" (Mark 1:15). There are saying-like statements about laws and rules (Mark 3:4; 7:15; Matt. 18:15-17) and the "I" sayings in which Jesus speaks of himself, his work, and his destiny (Mark 10:45; Matt. 5:17).

Although he did not write a body of specifically wisdom literature, Jesus continued the Hebrew wisdom tradition and was what we might call a sage. Unlike the teachers of his day, Jesus was not a Torah sage; he did not make it his teaching task to elaborate on Torah. He most often appealed to the world of human experience or made observations about nature, but he did so entirely within the typical forms of the earlier wisdom tradition. Harvey Cox places him directly within his cultural context by titling him Rabbi Yeshua ben Joseph, as I have invited Jewish readers to do.[19] Whatever additional identities or attributes are given him, we must acknowledge that he was thoroughly a part of his heritage and had integrated its style and focus into what he thought and said. Jesus seems to have had no other audience in mind than those who stood before him, although we find a timeless quality in his sayings. In the ancient Near East, "wisdom" denoted practical rather than abstract or theoretical knowledge, and it was this personal sort of wisdom that Jesus employed.

The gospel texts that seem most wisdomlike to us are the parables. C. H. Dodd provides an often-used but wordy description of a parable: "a metaphor or simile drawn from nature or common life, arresting the reader by its vividness or strangeness, and leaving the mind in sufficient doubt about its precise application to tease it into active thought."[20] That's a pretty good definition if you are patient enough to get through it. Use of the parable was certainly not original with Jesus. In using this form, he tapped into the wisdom tradition not only of Judaism, but also of other cultures of his day. In his hands the parable became a way of teaching that could get past the hearer's resistance and quickly present old ideas in a fresh framework. They invited listeners to see something they would not have seen, or would have resisted seeing, had the point been made directly. To put it bluntly, the hearer was blind-sided.

The prophets Nathan and Isaiah used this same approach. Nathan confronted King David with the story of the man who had only one ewe lamb. From David he got a verdict before David realized that the story applied to him (2 Sam. 12:1-6). Less well known but of the same genre is Isaiah's story about the vineyard that yielded wild grapes. Only after his hearers agreed that the vineyard should be pulled down did Isaiah say that the vineyard was Israel (Isa. 5:1-6). Both prophetic and wisdom traditions can be found in this story. It is exactly this sort of material that was Jesus' legacy, providing context for his view of the world and expression of his mission in it.

Jesus' Individuation of Spiritual Experience

It is what Jesus made of this legacy of prophecy and wisdom that now engages our attention. All of us, if we are to become fully developed people, take the material of our inheritance and fashion it into our own reality, reframing it to make the statement only we can make. Few people reach their individual potential, preferring instead to repeat the safer patterns of the past. *Only the person who chooses risk speaks an original word.*

Individuation as a Conscious Choice

As we look at the ways in which Jesus exhibits characteristics of an individuated person, it is important to clarify the term further, laying out what it does not mean. *Individuation* and the equally useful synonym *differentiation* do not imply opposition, to society or tradition. To say that a person has differentiated herself or has become individuated does not necessarily mean that she has been in rebellion against something, though indeed she may have been. Individuation is the process of becoming formed, of specializing within one's nature so as to become aware of one's individuality and recognizable personality. To be individuated is to become uniquely oneself, realizing one's innate capabilities.

   As we consider the spirituality of Jesus, we see that those things that make him a distinctive personality may or may not be against his tradition and culture. They may, indeed, be an integral part of his culture and inherited beliefs. Yet these elements would have been consciously chosen by him and intentionally incorporated, not assimilated lightly, without discrimination. Individuation is the recognition and choosing of personal identity, inherited or not.

In the interest of brevity, our focus here will be on two ways in which Jesus showed that he was individuated. To qualify as such, these behaviors would have been chosen from alternative ways of being that he did *not* select. Put more simply, individuation requires choice. Those choices need to be consistent and repeated so that what he claims to believe is congruent with his outward behavior. In summary, an individuating characteristic has two criteria: It is chosen over other available behaviors, and it is consistently evident in a lived-out fashion. Two individuating characteristics prominent in Jesus' life are *intentional spirituality* and *risk*. To explore these we will consider (1) his choice of the spiritual, interior life as his primary reality and (2) his decision to risk becoming an agent of change. We will examine these two characteristics with the understanding that they are conscious choices and not circumstantial accidents.

Choosing Spirit

Writing about individuation, French Dominican M. D. Chenu says that "each individual is radically insufficient in realizing his or her own nature fully. People are persons only in a community with all other persons."[21] Human individuation happens only within a human context. How would one know they were "other than" if there were no comparison available and no resistance for defining boundaries? It is out of Roman-period Judaism that Jesus defines himself, and it is within that framework that his choices are made. One of his choices is the decision to live by Spirit. According to the gospels, it was made at least as early as age twelve: "Why were you searching for me? Did you not know that I must be in my Father's house?" (Luke 2:49). Scholars give a great deal of attention to what Jesus said or did, but they seldom discuss what he *was* in an interior sense. We are uncomfortable with the subject of spirituality within ourselves and so avoid his. The modern church and modern theology are pervaded by the "practical atheism"[22] of our time. This way of seeing makes the assumption that there is no reality beyond the visible.

The visible world was just as palpable to Jesus as it is to all people.

Because of Judaism's preservation of its heritage, the world of Spirit was less hidden from Jesus than it is from us. Judaism suffered little from Hellenistic dualism, a view that separated the spiritual from the material world. Yet we are safe to say that many in his day, perhaps most, did not choose the life of Spirit. His parents seem to have chosen to hear the inner voice, but Jesus was surrounded, as are we, by those giving lip service to that voice. Jesus' choice of Spirit seems to be more a question of what we might now call the inner-directed life as opposed to the outer-directed life.

Within his world Jesus saw the emphasis on power, ownership, and fame that is evident in most cultures. As counterpoint, he had access to countless stories of the life of Spirit. He knew that Abraham saw visions and that Moses "knew God face to face" (Exod. 33:11 NIV). Both functioned as mediators between the world of Spirit and the people. Elijah was said to have traveled "in the Spirit" and was a mediator of God's power. Isaiah 6 details the stunning account of Isaiah's overwhelming experience of the spiritual world. And Ezekiel said, "The heavens were opened, and I saw visions of God" (Ezek. 1:1), while other prophets claimed that the Spirit of the Lord "fell upon them."

Although most people knew the stories, not all internalized the meanings, making them a real part of daily life. To many they were "long-ago" stories, just as they are to us now. One is not likely to have an experience of the Holy if one believes it not possible to do so. We can do only what we can first imagine. The much discussed Western poverty of spirit[23] may not be so much a consequence of accelerated knowledge as it is a dearth of imagination. Unlike Jesus, we live as orphans without a spiritual story.

As an adult Jesus carried out his earlier decision to live by Spirit. He sought the prophet John the Baptizer for affirmation and initiation then journeyed into the wilderness. In experiencing isolation and hunger, he had three visions. In what is often called the "vision quest," he made his decision not to live for bread, power, or fame. He would live by Spirit. It was a critical and highly individuating choice, one that affected everything that subsequently happened to him.

It is God-connection that marks a life of Spirit. As we noticed earlier, Jesus lived out a deeply prayerful life marked by an intense focus (seen in the Gethsemane prayer during which he sweat what appears to be blood) and intervals of solitude (seen in periodic retreats during his crowded ministry).

Within the vocabulary of spirituality and psychology, Rudolf Otto has made familiar the word *numinous*, by which he refers to the holy.[24] In conveying the power of presence of certain people, scripture often presents puzzling accounts of them having unusual powers and being accompanied by miraculous circumstance. We have no accurate idea of what the writers experienced. In reading the accounts as a group, it is clear that the authors are attempting to convey what Otto has called "the numinous." It makes far more sense to twentieth–century readers when we read that people around Jesus felt his authority and listened or obeyed. The gospel writers say that Jesus was experienced as a powerful presence. A personal numinous quality was marked by a quiet and awesome authority and power. We occasionally claim to have felt this quality in people of holiness, even today. We know it as a mark of the life lived in Spirit, one which has deeply developed over a period of time.

Choosing the life of Spirit is, in effect, addressing the inner part of one's world. The life of the Spirit was not only a passion that Jesus pursued for himself, but also a passion he desired for every person. But what of the outer life—that part lived in a sensory and circumstantial way? In examining the gospels it becomes clear that it was always Jesus' intention to influence, change, and affect those around him. Like the prophets who went before, he risked becoming mediator between the world of Spirit and the "world." There was always the nourishing and powerful tension between *being* and *doing*, between going inward and extending outward.

Jesus Chooses Change

Reliable scholarship contends that Jesus did not intend to found a religion outside Judaism. His concern was the renewal of Israel, and he saw his role as being prophetic. Historically the prophets had affirmed their tradition even as they sought to revitalize and transform it. Jesus' choice of twelve, not eleven or thirteen, disciples, was doubtless no accident. Twelve tribes made up the Israel he hoped to change. He seldom worked outside of national geographical boundaries. Even after his crucifixion, his following remained a Jewish revitalization movement until shortly after the destruction of the temple in C.E. 70. Paul did take the Christian story outside Jewish boundaries, but even he made very effort to preach first to Jewish communities.

What did Jesus want to accomplish? He preached about inner change. His agenda was transformation; his activity was lived-out compassion. Hebrew scripture speaks of God as being compassionate as well as holy. And Jesus placed his weight on the compassion of God. "Be compassionate, even as your Father is compassionate" (Luke 6:36).[25] (The words *perfect* and *merciful* are substituted in some translations.) His stories told about a prodigal son and the father who "had compassion," the Good Samaritan who "showed compassion," and about the unmerciful servant who did not. He healed on the Sabbath out of compassion and felt this action took precedence over any other consideration.

Heschel talks about the "pathos" of God, saying that God is not distant and unmoved, but that God feels for and with humankind.[26] Jesus' movement was about participation in the pathos of God as we understand it in Heschel's definition. He cared for the wealthy, the powerful, the helpless, and the poor. He ate and drank with tax collectors and outcasts and spoke to prostitutes and touched lepers. Jewish scholar Geza Vermes believes that Jesus' association with outcasts was the factor that differentiated him more than any other from his contemporaries and even his prophetic predecessors. Jesus, says Vermes, "took his stand among the pariahs of his world, those despised by the respectable."[27] The politics of compassion flew in the face of pockets of exclusivity, patriarchy, and the conflict with Rome. Jesus' attempt at creating an alternative community within first-century Judaism knew only limited success, but its creation seems to have been a risk he was determined to take.

What This Means for Us

As I've previously said, this book is written for readers interested in development of a personal spirituality or a corporate spirituality within the worshipping community. How is such formation accomplished? The how-to of such spiritual transformation is the difficult part. Gleaning from this discussion of Jesus, we note several things that promote growth in spirituality. Fortunately, many excellent, available books discuss the essentials for spiritual growth. And the spirituality typology based on integration and individuation presented in these pages is just another way to explore that growth. What we discuss here includes only a fraction of what can be said about spiritual formation. It is by no means the complete treatment. Rather, it is an understandable way to think about how we are the same as others, how we differ, and how we can enhance and enrich each other's spirituality. Relying on what we have observed about integration and individuation in the life of Jesus, we can now examine five attitudes and actions that contribute to a deepened and evolving spiritual life.

Being Willing to Change and Grow

The willingness to change and to grow is the foundation on which all else rests. This desire for more may be a burning passion, as described in the writings of the Desert Fathers and Mothers, or it may be a quieter and somewhat subtle wishing that has been with you for a while. There is no evident formula for making this willingness "appear." A simple interest in *seeing what is there* is motive enough to move.

Becoming Intentional

The second component of growth is the ability to point oneself in a direction. Again, *we can do only what we can first imagine.* Looking at the person of Jesus as model is a way of grasping what a fully developed spirituality looks like. "This is how it is done; this is how it looks." Most people acknowledge the importance of the models they had in childhood. The offspring of loud and blustery families are often loud and blustery as adults. Families where you never raise your voice or slam doors often have tip-toe children. When we daily see a modeling of certain behaviors, we tend to think that this is the way everyone, including ourselves, should behave. We point ourselves in the direction of our model. As for spirituality, we can choose Jesus as our model.

Integrating Tradition

A third component of spiritual growth is the ability to absorb and use the best that has come to us from others, past and present. We are at least inefficient and at most inexcusably blind if we treat casually those gifts of insight and learning that have been given by many who precede us. Understanding how to value tradition is one of our greatest resources. Politically we acknowledge that an American's disregard for the Constitution is disastrous, both for the person and for society. Spiritually we do equal damage when we take no notice of the writings and teachings of those who have formed our own religious traditions. Our refusal to integrate into our lives the best of our history is a depleting waste both for us individually and for the community.

So much for the past. It is even more difficult to integrate the gifts of others who are around us in the here and now. It's interesting that the things that first attract two people to each other, those ways in which they are *different* from each other, are the very features that most irritate those two people after they have been married two or three years. It is the same with religious groups and among people. The differences that at first fascinate us later become our reason for being "against" or for excluding. If I say my prayers spontaneously and extemporaneously, I may judge you to be "unspiritual" or "insincere" if you read yours. If you sing hymns with a beat and I prefer Bach or Handel, we may in time discover that we are not such close friends. After all, one of us has bad taste and the other is cold and uppity.

Pastoral counselor Howard Clinebell has written a list of features he believes characterize a healthy religion. He asserts that a beneficial religion will "build bridges rather than barriers between . . . persons with differing values and faith systems."[28] Inclusiveness, in other words, marks a wholesome faith stance. This does not imply a blanket acceptance of beliefs or practices from another faith discipline. It simply means that we accept that discipline as having value for those who are faithful to it and are open to the possibility that there may be something we can learn from another group. We face the fallacy in "Only me and mine have the complete and absolute truth."

Becoming an Individuated Person

The fourth component of spiritual growth (and psychological development) is individuation. Religious experience that encourages us to think for ourselves and appreciate the legacy of tradition promotes in us the fully developed personhood the Creator meant us to have. Clinebell's "healthy religion" list, mentioned above, includes the statement that religion should always "stimulate the growth of. . .inner freedom and autonomy."

A religion either does or does not cultivate within its followers a facility for listening to the inner voice. When the emphasis is only on the outer voice ("What you're told is all you can know"), the inner voice is silenced. There is little interior life, and if by chance there are stirrings and doubts, they are cause for guilt and hiddenness. Such religious expression does not trust God and what God might say to someone who does not hold established authority. This is exactly why they "stoned the prophets."

Becoming an Agent for Change

The fifth and final component to spiritual growth is the intention to effect change outside oneself. "Making a difference" is not where spiritual growth begins. Only after we have listened to the tradition and to our own sense of inner voice can we even guess what might be helpful. Many a disastrous crusade has been launched out of someone's hip pocket, without consultation with others and without benefit of one's interior knowing. There is an element of risk in wanting to effect change in the world. Those who rock the boat can get crucified or at least vilified, as we have observed. And then *not* doing something, or refusing to go on a crusade of doubtful merit, is equally courageous. Carrying out an action prompted by a sense of justice, kindness, compassion, or love causes spiritual growth-in-the-doing. It is the final fruit of all the preceding growth.

Summary

In summary, we begin the journey by wanting to grow then choosing a model or having a vision of who we want to be. As we progress, we take from the past and from others around us those elements that nourish and promote within us the life of Spirit. We experience the freedom to appreciate and the possibility to grow from other styles and ways. Further along in the journey, we begin to carve and shape our own individual spirituality. We learn to listen to and value our inner knowing, that part of us that is informed by all we have experienced so far and by the still, small Voice.

Here we have considered five actions that contribute to a deepened spiritual life. Now we will describe four different types of spirituality.

CHAPTER III

Four Types of Spirituality

In his book *A History of Christian Spirituality*, Urban T. Holmes explores a typology of spirituality. Actually, his comments cover only seven pages, but the ideas presented are so interesting and insightful that they bear a larger examination. He lays out a circle with two intersecting lines and labels the four lines with a type of spirituality.

My initial effort was to take Holmes's theory of spiritual type and make it more accessible to spiritual directors or people in spiritual direction. Although there are more than three hundred instruments designed to assess religious maturity,[1] there are few assessment tools that deal with spiritual type. As a clinical therapist, I often give an appropriate psychological assessment test to new clients. I have wanted just such an instrument to use for clients who come for spiritual companionship and guidance and those asking questions about their deeper spiritual needs.

Testing Holmes's Theory of Spiritual Type

I first tested Holmes's spirituality typology with my own clients and then conducted a year's testing with other individual people including spiritual directors and with several groups. To my surprise, I found the typology just as effective in determining group type as in testing individual type. Additionally, I saw a keen interest among all test subjects in comparing their personal spiritual type with that of their corporate spirituality; there was a fascination with the question "Are we a match?" In response to this interest, I developed the Spirituality Wheel Selector test to make such comparison easy.

In attempting to develop a test that reflected Holmes's philosophy, I saw that Holmes's theory did not adapt itself to the typical forced-choice testing to which we are accustomed. All our lives we have taken tests that instruct us to "choose *one* of these statements." Among Holmes's most important assertions is that people and groups have multiple spiritual tendencies, not just one. In other words, given a set of statements, I may feel that more than one of them is true of me. To make use of these ideas of spiritual type, the test had to be designed to permit selection of more than one statement. When testing the Spirituality Wheel Selector, I discovered that most people choose only one statement as expressive of their spiritual experience, which is a perfectly valid way to take it. Even so, to be accurate, a test appropriate to Holmes's theory must allow for several choices.

It is important to remember that Holmes insisted that each person and group has a *tendency toward favoring* one type of spirituality over other types. After taking the selector test, do not yield to the temptation to say, "I *am* a so-and-so-type spirituality," or, "I *am* a quadrant-2 type." Rather, see that you and your worshipping community are represented in several areas, with a strong tendency toward one of the four types.

Turn for a second to the Spirituality Wheel Selector test found on the last page of chapter 4. As we answer questions that place ourselves in the two circles, the congregational wheel and the individual wheel, we can see our place within a wider religious tradition, especially in regard to the ways we worship, meditate, and pray. Remember the statement by Chenu, quoted in the last chapter, that "each individual is radically insufficient in realizing his or her own nature fully. People are persons only in a community with all other persons." So it is that by comparing and seeing ourselves contextually that we recognize ourselves as unique and yet in some ways like others.

Placing "spokes" within a wheel was my solution for enabling the test taker to include his total spiritual expression. A forced-choice instrument would not have allowed this. In using a wheel, one may choose one or several or all of the statements presented. Each statement chosen is reflected as a spoke in the wheel. When finished, it is easy to see a real *picture* of who you are. The Spirituality Wheel is designed to draw your spiritual portrait.

What the Circle and Lines Mean

The use of two intersecting lines with the resulting quadrants has been used many times in the past, and I recently have seen two manuscripts for new books that employ this same useful format. The north-south and east-west poles of the two intersecting lines may carry any number of labels, depending on what you want to demonstrate. Holmes chose to designate four spiritualities. His line-scales are based on descriptive terms long available to theologians and observers of human nature. What is original, and so helpful to us, is his combining and configuring of these particular descriptions into a conceptual understanding of spiritual types.

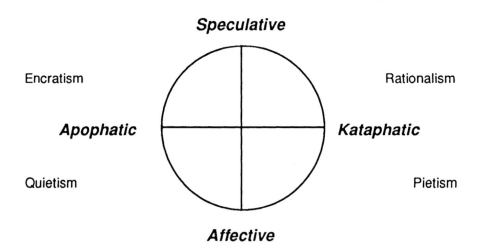

Adapted from *A History of Christian Spirituality* by Urban Holmes, II, 4. Copyright © 1980 by Urban Holmes, III. Reprinted by permission of Jane Holmes, Executrix.

The Circle

The circle itself represents the value placed on unity and on the interdependence of each part upon the other parts. Contained within the circle are the elements that make for wholeness and healthy spirituality. Holmes uses the word *sensibility* to describe one's awareness of the importance and contribution of the quadrants. This explains his name for the concept, the "Circle of Sensibility." By using this particular word he is saying that we are to become sensitive, that is *sensible*, to the differing styles of prayer, meditation, and spiritual expression. This, he says, promotes creative dialogue within the person and within the community.

The Vertical Scale: Speculative-Affective

The vertical axis of our circle is labeled speculative-affective with speculative being at the top or north of the circle. These two poles pose the question of how one goes about *knowing*—through the activity of the rational mind or by accessing feelings. "Head and heart" would be another less precise way of thinking of this scale. In this case *head* or *intellectual* or *cognitive* could substitute for *speculative. Heart* or *heart-felt* could be exchanged for *affective;* as used here, these words indicate knowing by feeling rather than by intellectualizing.

Both individual people and groups are inclined to gain their information about God, indeed about life in general, through (1) emphasizing logic and accumulated facts or (2) emphasizing instinct and intuitive feeling. Holmes says both modes—of learning and knowing—are needed by the worshipping community and by the people within it, though within any given group or particular person there will usually be a preference for one mode over the other.

The Horizontal Scale: Apophatic-Kataphatic

Here we have a mouthful! We seldom hear these two words used, but they are good ones to know. The horizontal scale is labeled apophatic-kataphatic with apophatic taking the left or west pole. By using these opposites, we are able to raise the question of how one conceptualizes

Divinity. The two poles present an *emptying* (apophatic) way of praying
and meditating or an *imaginal* or imagining (kataphatic) technique. I
have wished for more familiar words than these two. As you saw in
chapter 1, I present a second circle that substitutes the words *mystery* and
imaging, but these words are not as precise as Holmes's. Perhaps they
will help readers who just cannot swallow apophatic and kataphatic.

The Greek word *apophatikos* means "negative," and in Holmes's
schema it refers to the tendency of a person or a discipline to think of
God in nonconcretized ways; that is, to think of God as *mystery.* That
classic book of spiritual direction, *The Cloud of Unknowing,* is a perfect
example of this sort of thinking.

On the opposite end of this scale is the Greek word *kataphatikos,*
which is translated as "affirmative." It refers to the method of thinking
most familiar to Western culture, that of imaging God as revealed and
knowable. The Christian hymn "What a Friend We Have in Jesus" is a
natural expression of the kataphatic tendency to think of God in anthropomorphic images, in concrete terms—experiencing God both as friend
and as incarnate in the person of Jesus. (The ideas of viewing God with
and without image should not be confused with the use of symbol. Both
apophatic and kataphatic disciplines use symbol, but in different ways.)
My focus here is not on acts and objects that represent God, but on the
ways in which God is viewed in our minds.

Relationship to Myers-Briggs Categories

Those familiar with the Myers-Briggs categories might be tempted to
apply them to Holmes's schema.[2] I would urge some caution in doing
this. At first glance there seems a strong parallel between the types first
suggested by C. G. Jung and later developed by Isabel Myers, to those of
Holmes's circle. If one thinks of Jung's thinking-feeling (T-F) functions
as being comparable to Holmes's vertical speculative-affective axis, the
parallel is reasonable and even helpful. The intuitive-sensory (N-S)
preferences are not quite so close but are explanatory in understanding
Holmes's apophatic-kataphatic axis. It is my experience that further
comparisons break down. W. Paul Jones, professor of philosophical
theology at Saint Paul School of Theology in Kansas City and author of
articles on Myers-Briggs typology and its relationship to spirituality,[3]

believes Holmes's horizontal apophatic-kataphatic scale is somewhat but not absolutely parallel to the Myers-Briggs intuitive-sensing scale.[4] He advises against forcing too close a fit on the two typologies. If the Jungian categories are used, they should be limited to the four functions and placed at the poles of each axis, but they should not be used within the four quadrants. Making further comparisons is likely to distort both typologies.

Thinking in Two Different Ways

At this point let's take a parenthetical excursion to acknowledge that, as human beings, we are able to think in two quite different ways. This difference is somewhat parallel to the differences between *doing* and *being*. To understand the four spiritual types, it's important to understand the two ways of thinking. Contemporary research psychologist Robert Ornstein explains these two ways of thinking are complementary to one another. "One mode is verbal and rational, sequential in operation, orderly; the other is intuitive, tacit, diffuse in operation, less logical and neat, a mode we often devalue, culturally, personally, and even physiologically."[5] We might say that one is concrete and the other is mystical. Holmes refers to the two ways of thinking as the *receptive* mode and the *action* mode, and they become the tensions within his circle. A tension of opposites exists between any quadrant on the circle and its diagonal converse. We shall further explore this phenomena as we go along.

Holmes equates spiritual health with staying within the circle and in some way partaking of all its parts, if only in appreciating what the other quadrants offer. Holmes was influenced by the work of psychologist Arthur Deikman who postulated that mystical experience becomes possible only when we move out of the action, or kataphatic, mode of consciousness and into the listening or apophatic mode. Deikman says the receptive or listening mode is "a state organized around intake of the environment rather than manipulation" of the environment.[6] What a very un-Western thing to do; to take in the environment rather than to act on it or try to fix it! Keep in mind that the receptive mode is not a passive retreat from the environment, but an alternative strategy for engaging the world. This shift from the active to the receptive mode Deikman regards as essential to all mystic experience.[7]

Language, says Deikman, is the very essence of the action mode, in that we manipulate our environment through language strategies. Theology is often called our *reflection* on religious experience; it is not the experience itself. Theology, having to do with language, is "action." The mystical experience—experiencing the presence of God—is the complementary "receptive" component. Healthy interplay is created as one alternates between experience and reflection upon experience.

We can see that Western culture emphasizes analytical, reflective thinking while it neglects experiential awareness; we are inclined to think about God much more than to experience God's presence. This one-sided mode of gathering information limits our ways of knowing, making any mystic experience almost accidental.

Anthropologist Victor Turner, under whom Holmes studied, developed a parallel theory in which he says that human relationships fall into two types, "structure" and "anti-structure."[8] Structure and the action mode of consciousness are highly valued in institutions where order and predictability provide a sense of security. In such places we sense the fear that someone may do something untoward, or something embarrassingly out of line, God forbid! Holmes contends that to engage in deep, authentic prayer—a praying that is sensible to God and to all humankind—we must take the risk of moving into what Turner labels "anti-structure." This is similar to Deikman's insistence that the mystic experience can occur only in the receptive mode.

In reference to Turner's theories, we can point to the importance within Jewish and Christian spirituality of the wilderness or desert experiences. Exodus tells about all of Israel going into the desert. First Kings records a story of Elijah going into a cave in the wilderness and hearing "the still small voice" of God. We see in the life of Jesus this alternating from structure and engagement to nonstructure and retreat. The writings of the Christian mystics often come out of "the desert" and its antistructure context. Few among us have not spoken of or heard someone else refer to "the dark night of the soul."[9] Although John of the Cross was referring to a stage in the spiritual journey, we now take this phrase to refer to an experience marked by solitude and possibly loneliness coupled with a looking inward which, as John points out, is exactly what happens as one risks going into the spiritual unknown.

Holmes agrees with the value of wilderness passages in life. He quotes an Eskimo shaman speaking to the Danish explorer Rasmussen:

"All true wisdom is only found far from men, out in the great solitude, and it can be acquired only through suffering. Privations and sufferings are the only things that can open a man's mind to that which is hidden from others."[10] The virtue is not in suffering, *per se*; rather, suffering tears us away from the anesthetization of orderly comfort and forces us into the antistructure with its alternate mode of experiencing God.

And yet the familiar discursive ways of Western thinking have equal value. In this vein, Holmes commented that "Theology seeks to clarify the meanings of experience so that we may share the experience with our contemporaries and those who have gone before."[11] We need the words, the concrete records and history, to convey and interpret the experience of others. In other words, we need history. Scripture itself is the concrete, cognitive account of the deeply felt experiences of others. Without those accounts to furnish our minds, how else can we do what we have not yet imagined?

Abraham Maslow said, "If the only tool you have is a hammer, you tend to treat everything as if it were a nail."[12] Holmes invites us to consider using more than a single tool. We double our ability to know by using both our objective and subjective capabilities, rather than just the one in which we were trained. Psychologist Lawrence LeShan has observed that "each culture organizes its reality in a specific way, and its members are convinced that this is the only correct view of the universe."[13] It would be a shame to limp along with only one kind of perception. The spiritual types suggest to us the possibility of developing both kinds of thinking; of adding deepened dimension to spirituality, indeed, to all of life. In developing both apophatic and kataphatic experience, we enlarge our spiritual selves.

Four Spiritual Types

The vertical speculative-affective axis intersects with the horizontal apophatic-kataphatic axis forming quadrants. Within these quadrants, identified by the bordering poles, we find the four spiritual types. Quadrant 1, for instance, is influenced by the two points, speculative thinking and concrete (kataphatic) imaging of God. With the two bordering influences creating a particular spirituality, exactly what can we discover about spiritual type within all the quadrants? I suggest you read the following descriptions of the types now and again after you have taken the Spirituality Wheel Selector test.

At the conclusion of each description of the four spiritual types, I will address concerns of those called to do spiritual direction or who think of themselves as spiritual companions. These comments acknowledge the fact that each type of spirituality needs a different kind of nourishment.

Type 1:
Speculative/Kataphatic–A Head Spirituality

This is an intellectual "thinking" spirituality that favors what it can see, touch, and vividly imagine. Such concreteness could be theologically expressed in concepts, such as God as Father and/or Mother; for Christians, the centrality of Christ and the incarnation; for Jews, the Torah. What activities might this group ask for to enhance its spiritual life? Their choices will be based mostly on activity and on corporate gathering: more study groups, better sermons, and some sort of theological renewal within the worshipping community. (As you read further, you will notice that all four types seek renewal, but each seeks a different kind of renewal.) People in this group will support whatever helps them fulfill their vocation in life. The daily life, after all, is the "real world."

I was invited to lead a study for lay members and their pastors from three congregations of the same Christian denomination. After several hours of discussion of Holmes's "circle" concepts as they related to the groups' own printed orders of service and weekly newsletters, they agreed that their corporate worship expression fell predominantly within type 1 spirituality. It centered on gathering and the spoken word. To enrich their experience they needed to emphasize the opposite quadrant, type 3, fostering solitude, introspection, and silence. They planned a retreat, and then, in typical type-1 style, passed around a sign-up sheet, urging everyone to come. I expect the retreat ultimately featured a full program with little silence or solitude. If they did this, they were not "wrong"; they were simply exercising their style of spirituality. At some later time they may choose to risk the unstructured, the solitary, and the silent, but one sees the difficulty in doing what they could not, at that time, imagine.

The contribution of type-1 spirituality to the whole is invaluable. This style produces theological reflection and crafts position papers on ethical issues. It supports education and publication and causes us to examine the texts of our hymns to see if we are singing what we actually believe. Content is primary with this group, as is systematic congruence of thought and belief. While type 2 or 3 "experiences the Holy," it is type 1 that undertakes to make sense of that experience and to name it. They codify and so preserve the faith story from generation to generation; Bibles are read and Torah is studied. It is here that things are done "decently and in order," and we can be grateful for the coherence exerted on us all by the gifts of type 1.

Spiritual directors will discover they have fewer directees or companions from the type-1 group, which is prone to seek guidance chiefly from scripture and sermon—that is, from words. Yet some do seek spiritual guidance, and their particular needs must be understood in order for them to grow. Reading, journaling, and specific meditation with a definite focus are fruitful beginning activities. Prayer in this quadrant is almost always language or word-based prayer, whether aloud or silent. Theological discussion is usually easy with this type, but it is counterproductive to spiritual growth to allow all sessions to become "head trips." Growth for such people lies in their gradually sensing their interior connection with God. The goal, however, is to stretch experience, not to change style.

Holmes contended that any one of the quadrants could become so exclusively focused on its particular style that excess and aberration could occur, what Allan Sager calls "falling outside the circle."[14] For type 1, Holmes called this excess "rationalism." It is an overintellectualization of one's spiritual life with a consequent loss of feeling, often perceived as dogmatic and *dry*. The director will want to encourage flexibility and increased attention to the feeling and experiential side of spirituality.

Type 2:
Affective/Kataphatic—A Heart Spirituality

Notice that with type 2 we are still viewing God in kataphatic terms, but that we have dropped into the affective or lower half of the circle. This means type 2 is not a head-trip spirituality; it is all heart—combined with the concrete, real-life stuff. Here theology still emphasizes the anthropomorphic representation of God and the centrality of scripture, but this is now combined with a more affective, charismatic spirituality whose aim is to achieve holiness of life. The transformational goal is that of personal renewal.

It is interesting that national demographic figures indicate that the Christian population formerly concentrated in type-1 mainline denominations is now moving to no church membership at all or into congregations that represent type-2 experience.[15] One might conclude that there is a thirst for the affective in our lives, for an emotionally moving experience more in touch with feeling.

"While kataphatics of the mind may charge, 'My doctrine is purer than yours,' kataphatics of the heart counter with, 'My walk with the Lord is closer than yours.' "[16] It is an entirely different vocabulary based on whether one seeks illumination by rational mind or by heartfelt intuition. A type 2 will characteristically emphasize evangelism, since experience must be shared, and on transformation, sometimes of an obvious, even sudden type. Witnessing, testimonials, and especially music mark corporate worship. Theologically this experience stresses the immanence of God over the transcendence of God. God is real in the here and now, and, as the rhythmic gospel chorus says, "Yes, God is real, 'cause I can feel him deep in my soul!"

Type-2 prayer is made with words but the words are used less formally than with type 1, and praying is usually extemporaneous. These people focus on personal service to others but often with the caveat that the service provide opportunity to witness about one's faith. Witness and proclamation are so important to type 2 that they often use mass media, such as television and radio, even creating their own national and worldwide media networks. Their contribution to the whole is the warmth of feeling, energy, and freedom of expression others sometimes lack. African-American churches, especially, have this capacity for spontaneity and ebullient spirituality.

Spiritual direction of the type-2 person may begin with the story of her life told from a spiritual perspective and a relating of these events to the biblical story. Such people may respond well to a loosely structured daily spiritual discipline. They often need permission to acknowledge anger, disappointment, sadness, and doubt, and to allow themselves to be less than ideal. Their spirituality is enriched by being able to see expressions of faith other than their own as having value and making contribution. You might also encourage type 2 directees to risk new experience on their own and to trust God to be with them in their journeys, seeing God as the nurturing rather than the punitive parent.

Holmes calls the excess for this group "pietism." The focus can become too exclusive, resulting in an "it's us against the world" mentality that does not acknowledge the spiritual experience of others, especially if it differs in any way from a type-2 experience. Spirituality in this quadrant is sometimes disdained for being too emotional and for believing that an affective experience must be duplicated in others if the experience of these others is to count as valid. These people may be viewed as anti-intellectual if their exclusivity results in being closed to the risk of new thought.

Type 3:
Affective/Apophatic—A Mystic Spirituality

In type 3 we are still within affective, or feeling, experience, but we move for the first time into apophatic knowing. Here *hearing from* God rather than *speaking to* God is prominent. The aim of this spirituality is union with the Holy, and, although this is never completely achievable, only the continued attempt, or "the journey," satisfies. People attracted to this type of spirituality are often by nature contemplative, introspective, intuitive, and focused on an inner world as real to them as the exterior one. This is most often the home of the mystic.

Instead of a God who possesses characteristics similar to human ones, God is ineffable, unnameable, and more vast than any known category. God's statement to Moses, "I AM WHO I AM" (Exod. 3:14), makes perfect sense to a type-3 person and is accurate to his understanding of the Holy. A life of austerity and asceticism is appealing to many in this quadrant—not because they are necessarily self-punishing, but because simplicity of life quiets outside distractions and enables one to attend more fully to the inner voice. People of this spirituality often find themselves uncomfortable and not fitting in, especially within Western Protestantism or within synagogues that are primarily cultural assemblies. They will discover the works of writers such as Anthony de Mello[17] and Thomas Merton[18] and feel that they are like thirsty survivors of the desert who have come upon water. Jewish readers may rediscover the Kabbalah,[19] or enjoy the writings of contemporary writers such as Lawrence Kushner.[20] If they leave organized religion, and frequently they do, they may be attracted to Eastern religions because of the apophatic approach (a former emphasis of Christianity and Judaism that has largely been discarded in Western technological culture). Their agenda is renewal of inner life.

Theologically people on the apophatic side tend to see God as

Creative Force and may be attracted to a creation–type theology.[21] Those of a slightly different bent may enjoy reading the work of Alfred North Whitehead, although the appeal of his work is certainly not limited to just one quadrant.

The type-3 contribution to the whole of spiritual experience is enormous. Many in this group write and publish and provide the especially inspirational and uplifting spirituality that fuels our daily lives with a sense of the Holy. Type-3 spirituality provides fodder for much of the intellectual interpretation and theological writing done by type 1. These are the people who push the frontiers of spirituality, enabling us to imagine what we might do if we would be open enough.

To a spiritual director the spiritual needs of a type-3 person are usually evident, and fortunately people from this sector frequently seek spiritual direction. As those from type 2 need permission to be human, those from type 3 need permission to retreat and seek solitude. They may have bought into the American myth that says being alone and doing "nothing" is lazy, antisocial, and unproductive. They may feel guilty and odd as they carefully hide their desire for the nourishment of solitude and silence. Once they have realized who they are and become comfortable with their spirituality, type-3 people are more likely to laugh than any other group. Remember Saint Francis of Assisi? Truly a laughing mystic.

The excess of this quadrant is labeled "quietism," an aberration that leads to exaggerated retreat from reality and from interaction with the world. Quietism tends to spiritual passivity rather than initiative and deprives the world of the treasured gifts of mysticism. The mystic who lacks the balance of the other spiritual expressions is also deprived of the blessing of interaction with others and the lessons provided by friction. Unless it is discerned that they have a true vocation for solitary prayer, and some do have such a calling, spiritual direction will steer these people to alternating their retreat time with involvement and interaction. Teaching techniques of meditation and contemplation are especially fruitful.

Type 4:
Speculative/Apophatic—A Kingdom Spirituality

Type 4 is the smallest group. Because there are relatively few examples, it is the most difficult to describe. The mystic, apophatic experience coupled with an intellectual mode of gathering data makes for an active visionary who is single-minded with a deeply focused, almost crusading, type of spirituality. When we try to envision this quadrant, we think less of denominations or faith groups and more of individual people. In fact, people of this spiritual type care less about affiliation with organized religion than do many others, certainly less than those in types 1 and 2. Their aim is simply to obey God and to witness to God's coming reign. Theirs is a courageous and sturdy idealism that takes responsibility for change; they have a passion for transforming society. While type 3 tends toward retreat, the type 4 is inclined to be assertive, even aggressive, in desire to implement a vision of the world as the kingdom of God on earth.

I have no idea what Ralph Nader's spiritual life may be like, but politically he perfectly exemplifies this single-minded dedication of the intellectual visionary. From a faith standpoint, these people frequently sacrifice their personal lives for their hope that the kingdom will be realized on earth; they may even become martyrs to their cause. The Hebrew prophets and the Apostolic Fathers and Mothers come to mind in thinking of type 4 as well as Savonarola, Joan of Arc, Martin Luther, John Calvin, Dorothy Day, Elie Wiesel, and the spirit found in present-day liberation theology. For these people the regeneration of society becomes a personal crusade, fueling a strong desire to rectify the wrongs of the world.

They equate prayer and theology with action. It is not uncommon to hear statements such as, "My work and my prayer are one," or, "I pray with my hands and feet." Their gifts to us are tremendous—found in the

freedom marches of the sixties and overseas in the Peace Corps. They
lead us in the difficult and embarrassing issues, caring little about how
others may judge them. They have their vision of the ideal, and your
opinion and mine will hardly matter when placed alongside that vivid
driving image.

Spiritual guidance offered to such a person should channel and interpret—not stifle—the evident spiritual energy. Respectfully listen to
anger and exasperation with authority figures, being patient and firm in
your response. Encourage small-group support and alternative modes of
worship if the present style is not affirming. For type 4 the growing edge
is the knowledge that God has ultimate control; although they may offer
their considerable gifts, they do not need to be "driven" to be faithful.
These people need to hear the words of the fourteenth-century English
mystic Julian of Norwich: "But all shall be well, and all shall be well,
and all manner of thing shall be well."

An excessive and unbalanced spirituality in this type is called
"encratism" and refers to a moralistic and unrelenting tunnel-vision. If
you are not supporting "the cause" with the same selfless effort that they
expend, you are not a part of their world. In her single-mindedness, a
type 4 may not notice you. Do you know a person with strong type-4 tendencies? He can trouble our lives, even make us feel guilty, but we find
ourselves admiring this person for being willing to make a difference.

The Circle as Invitation to Spiritual Wholeness

The primary value of this approach to spiritual type is not in being able
to pigeonhole oneself or other people or groups, saying, "I *am* this category or type." Such an application undermines the core of Holmes's
meaning by suggesting limitation rather than latitude. Rather, the typology shows that we all have tendencies toward certain ways of living out
our spirituality and that our growing edge is the tension placed on us by
"the other." Of necessity, the above descriptions of four types are over-
drawn. We could safely guess that almost no one falls entirely into one
quadrant or type of spiritual expression without any shade or inclination
toward at least one other type.

The message of Holmes's circle is this: Once we have found where
we fall within the total circle, we then have opportunity to grow by

(1) acknowledging and strengthening our present gifts, (2) growing toward our opposite quadrant, and (3) appreciating more perceptively the quadrants on either side of our dominant type. Worshipping groups will want to plan to meet the needs of more people by stretching toward some variety of expression without losing the central identity of the group. People who find their spirituality represented in several quadrants may be encouraged to see that they are capable of several kinds of worship experience.

From several constructs and typologies that provide ways of seeing spirituality, I have chosen to explore this particular schema because (1) it offers a template by which basic spiritual types can be affirmed, while it provides (2) spiritual tension from alternate styles encouraging a path toward wholeness. Presentations of spirituality are often hierarchical, with one expression viewed as being higher or better than another. We get competitive about that sort of ranking and defeat our own best interest by forcing on ourselves things we do not really feel. In Holmes's schema of spirituality, each category is of value, yet all are different.

I encourage you to work with these ideas. They will foster growth through the individuation of your personal spirituality and enrich you as you integrate into your life the experience of others. Using this typology, we each come to know more truly our own gifts and to see their value to corporate spiritual life. The Spirituality Wheel Selector test is designed to affirm gifts and to reveal differences, not to evaluate the maturity or worth of any particular spiritual style.

We have discussed the importance of integrating all the types of spirituality to make for a balanced whole. We have also discussed the equal importance of becoming individuated, of recognizing our own individual spiritual type as indicated by the combinations that create the four spirituality types. We are now ready to use the Spirituality Wheel with some deeper understanding, appreciating the meaning of its results to our own experience.

CHAPTER IV

Using the Spirituality Wheel Selector

Look ahead to the end of this chapter, to the Spirituality Wheel Selector test. You will see that it shows two wheels, or circles, one labeled "congregational style" and one labeled "personal style." The wheels themselves are identical and marked with the two axes identified by characteristics of spirituality. Each quadrant, or spirituality type, is numbered. As you take the test, you will consider statements from twelve categories. By drawing into the wheels spokes that describe you (or your congregation), you identify your profile.

As placed on one page, these circles enable you to see how your own individual style matches with the spiritual style of your worshipping group. As the two styles emerge, much as a portrait does as the artist paints it, you will be able to compare them. I trust the comparison will explain much about your feelings that surface as you participate in congregational worship.

Just before the test page you will find statements that identify the wheels' "spokes." The first set of statements, for example, has to do with "order of service." Statement 1 is indicative of a type-1 spirituality: intellectual (speculative) types who tend to see God in concrete terms (kataphatic). Statement 2 typifies a type-2 spirituality, seeing God in concrete terms but screened through the "heart" rather than the "head." Statement 3 is a reflection of type-3 spirituality, the mystic style. The fourth statement is the attitude expressed by a type-4 spirituality, which engages in visionary action.

What if you read the statements and discover that more than one of them reflects your spiritual feeling or your experience? You may even feel that all four are expressions you would claim. If that's the case, draw a spoke into each quadrant you choose. That is what makes this method of test-taking different. You are not limited to one choice only, even as you are not limited in your expression of the spiritual. Here is what a circle might look like when it is finished.

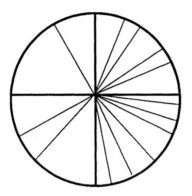

The next thing to consider is how to take the selector test, first for your congregation and then for yourself. As you read the first set of statements, look at the upper circle and ask yourself, "Is this the way my congregation feels about this?" Or, "Does this statement reflect what my congregation thinks is important?" If the answer is yes, draw a spoke or a line into the quadrant that matches the statement number.

Before going to the next set of statements, *read the same set of statements again*, asking yourself, "Is this the way *I* feel about this?" Or, "Does this statement reflect what is important to *me?*" Enter your affirmative responses on the lower wheel.

Now go on to the second set of statements and go through the process again. There are twelve sets of statements in all.

What if you come to a set of statements and find that you do not claim any of the four? Then enter no spokes into the wheel you are working with. Whatever you *do* and *do not* choose is an important part of the testing information.

I have been giving the Spirituality Wheel instrument for some time now and have noticed that once participants adjust to the test style, they move easily through the sets of questions. There may be a few who have a difficult time at first, simply because it is an unfamiliar method of evaluating. Many have whispered to me, "I don't think you realize it, but the test gives away the answers." Yes, it does. Why should anyone lie?

We are trying to determine one among equally valuable styles. Again, this does not have correct or incorrect answers. All statements reflect the legitimate feelings of various people.

Most people who have had difficulty have said, "I can't decide which statement to choose; I feel several of them are true." Then make a spoke for all the statements you feel are true for you, or for your congregation. Remember, this is not a forced-choice instrument! I certainly would have preferred a forced-choice test because they are so familiar and everyone knows how to take them. But one of the most important features of Holmes's work—one with which I strongly agree—is that we are not just one exclusive type. Our spirituality is fed by many influences, as well as by our own complex temperaments. An accurate testing of spiritual type will need to accommodate that complexity and variety.

If you follow the instructions exactly, you will quickly get the hang of it. I think you will discover that your individual and corporate spiritual tendencies are fairly portrayed in the pictures that emerge. I have observed that once people are into the test, they want to continue talking and discussing—all the way out the door.

Because of the differences in language and some difference in custom, I have made slight alterations in the basic selector test to accommodate Roman Catholic and Jewish readers. You may wish to take the basic test, whatever your faith group. You will find the Roman Catholic and Jewish test adaptations in the appendix. I hope you enjoy them. I will welcome your comments as to how they can be improved for future use.

One other note before you start. After you have taken the selector test, you may see it as a valuable and interesting workshop for a group in your church or synagogue. To accommodate this interest, you have permission to photocopy the test pages for group use. You may want to enlarge the photocopy if your copier has that capability. Even though you furnish test sheets to the group, each person attending a workshop should have her own book, since the workshop plans in chapters 5 and 6 rely on reading assignments from the text. These chapters will help you plan and conduct a workshop that fits your needs.

(To see a sample of how a finished, filled-in wheel might look, see the illustration in chapter 6 under the heading "Using the Data.")

The Spirituality Wheel©
A Selector for Spiritual Type

Basic Test

Corinne Ware, D. Min.

The purpose of this exercise is to DRAW A PICTURE of your experience of corporate worship and compare it to the picture of your own personal style of spirituality.

Before you start, look at the last page of the test. You will see two circles, each divided into quadrants numbered 1, 2, 3, and 4. Each quadrant stands for a type of spiritual expression. In the top circle, you will "draw a picture" of spiritual experience in your particular congregation. In the bottom circle, you will "draw a picture" of your personal style.

Congregational Style

Read through the first set of statements (starting below) and select the one(s) that describe what you do in your worshipping group. *You may select none or more than one if you wish.* Notice the number that goes with your chosen statement. On the *top* wheel on the last page of the test, find the numbered quadrant that matches the number of your chosen statement. In that quadrant draw a line (a spoke going from the center to the outside edge of the circle). If you've chosen two statements, draw two spokes, each in a different quadrant. Before you go on to the next set of statements, fill in the "personal style" wheel for the first set.

Personal Style

Read through the first set of statements a second time. Now choose the statement or statements that describe what you *personally* prefer as part of your spiritual experience. *You may select one statement or more than one.* Match the chosen statement number with the quadrant number in the lower circle. In that quadrant draw a spoke-line. If you've chosen two statements, draw two spokes, each in a different quadrant. The result is a portrait of your personal style, which you can compare with the experience you have in your worship group.

THE ORDER OF WORSHIP

1. A carefully planned and orderly worship program is a glory to God.
2. A deeply moving and spontaneous meeting is a glory to God.
3. Simplicity and some silence are important elements needed for worship.
4. It is not a service, but ordering ourselves to God's service that is important.

TIME

1. Stick to announced beginning and ending times of worship services.
2. It is important to extend the meeting time if one feels led to do so.
3. All time is God's time. A sense of timelessness is important.
4. Gather whenever and as long as you need to in order to accomplish the task.

PRAYER

1. Words express poetic praise; we ask for knowledge and guidance.
2. Let words and feelings evoke God's presence in this moment.
3. Empty the mind of distractions and simply BE in the presence of the Holy.
4. My life and my work are my prayer.

MUSIC

1. Music and lyrics express praise to God and belief about God.
2. Singing warms and unites us and expresses the soul's deepest heart.
3. Chant and tone bring the soul to quietness and union with God.
4. Songs can mobilize and inspire to greater effort and dedication.

PREACHING

1. The Word of God, rightly proclaimed, is the centerpiece of worship.
2. The gospel movingly preached is the power of God to change lives.

3. Proclamation is heard when the Spirit of God speaks to the inward heart.
4. What we do is our "preaching" and speaks louder than anything we say.

EMPHASIS

1. A central purpose is that we fulfill our vocation (calling) in the world.
2. A central purpose is that we learn to walk in holiness with the Lord.
3. A central purpose is that we be one with the Creator.
4. A central purpose is that we obey God's will completely.

SUPPORT OF CAUSES

(If necessary, circle the words that apply and select categories with the most circles.)

1. Support seminaries, publishing houses, scholarship, preaching to others.
2. Support evangelism, missions, spreading the word on television and radio.
3. Support places of retreat, spiritual direction, liturgical reform.
4. Support political action to establish justice in society and its institutions.

CRITICISM

1. Sometimes we (I) are said to be too intellectual, dogmatic, and "dry."
2. Sometimes we (I) are said to be too emotional, dogmatic, anti-intellectual.
3. Sometimes we (I) are said to be escaping from the world and are not realistic.
4. Sometimes we (I) are said to have tunnel vision and are too moralistic.

DOMINATING THEMES

(If necessary, circle the words that apply and select categories with the most circles.)

1. Discernment, discipline, knowledge, order, grace, justification.

2. Love, conversion, witness, spontaneity, sanctification.
3. Poverty, humility, wisdom, letting go, transcendence.
4. Simplicity, purity of heart, action, temperance, obedience, martyrdom.

MEMBERSHIP CRITERIA
(What the congregation believes is necessary; what you believe is necessary.)

1. Assent to doctrine, baptism, endorsement by group.
2. A personal inward experience of God, baptism, public declaration.
3. All who face Godward are incorporated in the Holy.
4. Solidarity with humankind is membership in God's kingdom.

RITUAL AND LITURGY

1. Ritual and liturgy evoke memory and presence, teaching traditional truths.
2. Liturgy and ritual ceremonies are not of great importance.
3. Ritual and liturgy are ways in which God becomes present to us.
4. Ritual and liturgy are one way we make statements about inner conviction.

CONCEPT OF GOD

1. God is revealed in scripture, sacrament, and in Jesus Christ and his cross.
2. I can feel that God is real and that Christ lives in my heart.
3. God is mystery and can be grasped for but not completely known.
4. We participate in the mystery of God when we become co-creators with God in the world.

The Spirituality Wheel©
A Selector for Spiritual Type

Corinne Ware, D. Min.
Based on the spirituality typology by Urban T. Holmes

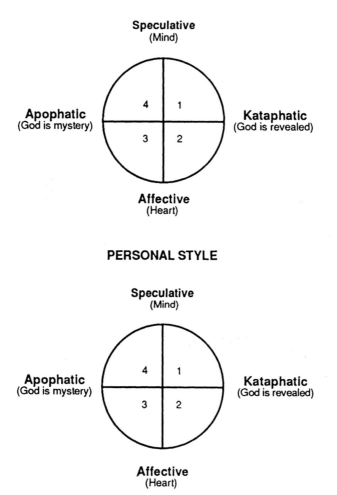

CONGREGATIONAL STYLE

Speculative
(Mind)

Apophatic
(God is mystery)

Kataphatic
(God is revealed)

Affective
(Heart)

PERSONAL STYLE

Speculative
(Mind)

Apophatic
(God is mystery)

Kataphatic
(God is revealed)

Affective
(Heart)

Adapted from *The History of Christian Spirituality: An Analytical Introduction* by Urban T. Holmes. © The Seabury Press. Used by permission of Jane N. Holmes, Executrix.

CHAPTER V

Workshops for Congregations

This chapter is written for congregational leaders who want to better understand their communities of worshippers. Maybe you feel pressure to change some of the worship patterns, to add or subtract organizational programs, or to hire new staff members. A clearer picture of the congregation as a whole will inform any such change and help avoid errors that create disappointment and loss of energy.

Readers who are interested only in enhancing their own personal spirituality, or one-on-one spiritual directors, may want to skip some parts and move on to chapter 6.

Formats for Group Use

Initially you will want to determine your ultimate goal in conducting a group study of spiritual type. If you want to learn about the nature and characteristics of the entire worshipping community, consider an all-congregation survey. If your goal is to get congregational members to grapple with their own and the congregation's spiritual identity, you may wish to use a small-group format. Maximum benefit, however, will come when you use both the large-group survey *along with* additional small discussion groups. I suggest you hold small-group meetings following the general survey. In this way, the small group(s) can reflect on the large-group results, interpreting both corporate and personal type.

Leading a Large Group in Using the Spirituality Wheel

The advantage in testing the entire group at one time is that you will get the big picture. You will have concrete data on the characteristics of your particular congregation. The disadvantage is that this large-scale approach, when used alone, will not prompt the discussion, analysis, and understanding that small groups generate. This is why you may wish to follow the congregational testing with small-group meetings for those interested in continuing the study.

If you decide to give the Spirituality Wheel Selector test to the congregation gathered in one place, reserve twenty to thirty minutes for the exercise—to give directions and administer the test (and answer questions during the test). You may have completed the test in a much shorter time, but do not assume that others will fall into line with complete understanding. Some people take tests better than others, and, as I have said before, it takes a little time to acclimate oneself to taking any test that is neither essay nor forced choice.

I suggest you use a chalkboard or poster drawing to demonstrate how a *completed* test might look. For ease in tallying group responses, a test taker should add up the number of spokes in each quadrant and write this number outside the circle. Draw your own test, if you wish, and use it as a sample. This usually solves any problems.

When you gather and tally the results, plan a time within the following two weeks to explain to that same group the meaning of what they have done. A sermon or talk that addresses the "who are we?" question generates interest and discussion. Emphasize the strengths of the congregation as well as pointing out its possible growing edge. Chapter 6 will explain more about how to interpret the data you gather and will guide in shaping a constructive response. You might distribute an enlarged version of the completed congregational wheel, as shown in chapter 6. It is helpful to have this visual presentation when explaining the results.

Leading a Small Discussion Group

You may choose to combine your survey with a small-group study, or you may prefer to have a small-group study alone without the general survey. Consider planning a one-week (four sessions; Monday through

Thursday) or two-week (eight sessions) workshop for your group(s). A one-day plan is also easy to facilitate (see heading below). The material included for study can be adapted to all sorts of time frames to suit your particular circumstance.

To provide a framework, let's look at a short, one-week workshop of six hours (four sessions, ninety minutes each), and a longer, two-week workshop of twelve hours. The two-week study explores all you have read in this book. Sessions are designed so that a group doing a four-session workshop can elect to extend their meetings an additional four sessions. Groups frequently become invested in learning about themselves and want to explore further. If possible, leaders should leave some open time, allowing for that possibility.

You may form one discussion group or several. To facilitate a maximum exchange of ideas, any group should probably have no more than eight people. Meetings could take place in a home or in the church or synagogue building. What counts is not where it is held so much as how it feels: not so large a room as to dwarf the group and not so small as to feel crowded. Most groups work best when a little "hospitality" is offered, such as coffee and donuts. Once you plan anything more ambitious in the way of food, you can lose the working mother, the single man, or the noncompetitive cook—people whose ideas are important to the group.

Allow ten minutes for arrivals, eating, and getting settled; then start on time. More important, end the meeting at exactly the time announced. People inclined to continue the discussion after the meeting is over can do so in the hallway, the parking lot, or over more coffee. Others may be meeting a bedtime deadline or getting home to the baby–sitter. People should always be able to exit at the agreed–upon time.

Leading a One-Day Study

If your group is best suited for a one-day (Saturday?) workshop, use the shorter four-session plan outlined below, with sessions 1 and 2 in the morning, and 3 and 4 after lunch. Note that for session 3, you can omit the opening summary and the ten minutes allotted to each session for getting refreshments and getting settled. This will net you about twenty-five minutes, and you can easily have a one-day workshop that starts at nine, breaks at noon for a one-hour lunch, and ends at 3:30 p.m. Encourage everyone to dress casually and make lunch fun and easy.

Christian and Jewish Congregations

Because a Christian service of worship and a Jewish service have so many elements in common, I have tried to keep both groups in mind in applying Holmes's typology. The suggestions made here will probably fit best with the Reform Jewish tradition, though they can be adapted to others. There is a growing group of deeply spiritual people within Judaism who see their worship affiliation as more than the preservation of culture, as valuable as that function is. One has only to look at lists of recently published books to see that this group is tapping into the spirituality of Judaism, returning to the deep and nourishing roots of faith. The spirituality types presented here can help these people to identify their own spiritual natures, and understand how it is that they can grow within the context of their own tradition.

Christendom comprises many denominations and groups, and nearly all have developed liberal and conservative subgroups. Given a choice, we tend to gravitate to the type of worship that appeals to our inner spiritual need. That in itself explains much about the existence of denominations in the first place. Many people who seek spiritual counseling do so because they have grown up in a denomination or worship group that, while admirable, does not "fit" them or meet their deepest needs. The effort here is not to encourage church swapping on a mass scale. I believe, however, that we must be interested in people's natures and needs and stop assuming that what works for one is the formula for all. Once people understand these deep and personal needs, they often can adjust their lives to include experiences that supplement and enhance their connection to God. They may well decide to remain within their original faith groups while owning their right to seek what they need at this particular point in their journeys.

Denominations themselves have characteristics of spiritual type. Several mainline Protestant groups represent an emphasis on the speculative or intellectual style. While one will find a warm, heartfelt faith in almost all denominations, we are not surprised to find it most often in evangelical groups. And then there are churches where, upon entering the building or hearing the music, one feels the sense of the sacred and of mystery. How can it all occur within the same faith? We have many riches to share.

Now that I have outlined approaches for your congregation or group, let's continue with guidance in presenting the material. When you are asking somebody to be the leader of a workshop group, it helps to be able to say, "Look, here's an outline showing you exactly what to do." She may of course modify the outline or change the arrangement of the material altogether. Most of us have a sneaking fear that we will not be able to fill up the time. But generally discussions of the Spirituality Wheel and its concepts not only fills but exceeds the allotted time. Your problem will most likely be one of controlling the discussion so that the material is covered.

Study Guide for a Four-Session Workshop

You may be thinking about giving the leader a copy of this book and providing only selector-test copies for the group participants. I strongly suggest that each participant have his own book, whether or not you use separate tests. In the following presentation I assume that everyone will have access to a book; I will suggest the appropriate chapter to read for each session.

Session 1:
Introducing the Spirituality Typology and Taking the Test

A week before session 1, distribute the books and ask participants to read the preface and chapter 1 as preparation.

For session 1 there are two goals: to explain the spirituality types and to have group members complete both wheels on the Spirituality Wheel Selector test.

If the test has already been given to the entire congregation, people will still need to complete a copy for the group sessions. (In most cases the congregational copies will have been collected.)

For session 1 have available a chalkboard or flipchart to draw the circle and label its intersecting lines. During the session, the concept of the circle and its lines will be covered briefly. A review will follow in session 2, so do not worry if you have to rush through the first time you explain it. Here is a session outline you can follow.

10 min.	Greetings, refreshments
10 min.	Introduction
	• Say why you believe there is value for this group engaging in the study.
	• Ask impressions of those who have read the book preface and chapter 1.
	• Briefly review questions the selector test will answer (see chapter 1).
10 min.	Explain the concept of the circle (see chapter 1).
	• Discuss the value of a balanced whole that represents healthy spiritual life.

15 min.	Explain the four poles of the two lines that divide the circle (see chapters 1 and 3).
	• Speculative
	• Affective
	• Kataphatic
	• Apophatic
15 min.	Explain the quadrants bounded by two characteristics (see chapter 3).
	• Type 1: Speculative-Kataphatic
	• Type 2: Affective-Kataphatic
	• Type 3: Affective-Apophatic
	• Type 4: Speculative-Apophatic
10 min.	Break
20 min.	Take the Spirituality Wheel Selector test (see chapter 4).
	• Explain that more than one spoke can be drawn for each set of statements.
	• Some may wish to count the number of lines in each quadrant for comparison.
	• Ask the group to reflect on what was learned and be ready to comment further at the next session.

Assign reading of chapter 3 for next session.
Dismiss

Session 2:
Teaching the Circle Concepts

Session 1 was almost too much to absorb. By now, members of the group have had time to think about their tests and have begun to wonder, *Now what did so–and–so mean*? Introduce session 2 by quickly review-ing the session–1 outline. Then ask for feedback on what each person has learned from his or her "portraits."

10 min.	Greetings, refreshments
10 min.	Review the circle and its intersecting lines. Use a chalkboard.
	• Answer remaining questions about the concepts.
30 min.	Lead a discussion about what each has learned from the Spirituality Wheel. *Discussion questions about you:*

	• What did you discover about yourself that you did not know?
	• What strengths does the test say you have? Does the group agree?
	• Where is your "growing edge" (your opposite quadrant)?
	• Did you find an excess in your life?
10 min.	Break
30 min.	Continue discussion. *Discussion questions about the congregation:*
	• In what ways are you and the congregation a "fit"?
	• In what ways different? Were any unmet needs discovered?
	• What is the chief strength of the congregation?
	• Is your spirituality accepted and used by the congregation?
5 min.	Explain the meaning of the term *lectio divina* (see chapter 8).

Assign reading of chapter 8 for next session. Ask participants to bring their books to session 3.

Dismiss

Session 3:
Experiential Learning with *Lectio Divina*

Prepare for this session by reading chapter 8.

This session provides one of the most enjoyable activities of the series and a break from the focused discussion and study of the spiritual types.

The purpose of session 3 is to put into practice what has been learned. Group members can experience for themselves just how their spiritual types influence the way they read scripture.

Have available Bibles or photocopies of the passage you wish to study. Participants will work from "A Short Guide to *Lectio Divina*," found on the last page of chapter 8. (Have photocopies of that page available.) In chapter 8 find general suggestions for suitable scripture selections. You might enjoy using the story of Esther, focusing on Esther 4:13-16. Suggested New Testament selections: Peter's dream in Acts 10:9-16 or the Good Samaritan story, Luke 10:30-37. Decide on one passage that suits your group's interest or needs at this time and use it for the study. Whichever scripture passage you choose, everyone *must work with the same selection* so that discussion and exchange of experiences can take place.

As leader you may be tempted not to participate in the exercise with the group. I urge you to join in the experience. Just keep your wristwatch in view and trust yourself to remain aware of the time. Without engaging in the experience, you cannot really participate in the discussion that follows. Here is an outline that will guide you through the revealing experience of *lectio divina*.

10 min.	Greetings, refreshments
10 min.	Briefly review the history and purpose of *lectio divina* (see chapter 8).
	• Make sure everyone is comfortable and ready to enter deeply into the experience.
15 min.	Give each person a copy of the scripture selection. Guide the group through the process below a step at a time until all four steps are completed.

1. Begin by quietly reading aloud the *lectio* paragraphs and asking if there are questions. Allow silent time for all to read the scripture passage.

2. Without discussion, continue by reading aloud the *meditatio* paragraph. Ask if there are any questions. Allow time for all to read the scripture passage again.

3. Without discussion, read aloud the *oratio* paragraph and ask if there are questions. Allow time for all to scan the scripture passage a third time.

4. Without discussion, read aloud the *contemplatio* section, asking for questions. This will be the most difficult way of reading formost in your group. If the group is large enough, one or two may take to it easily.

10 min.	Break
15 min.	Ask for feedback from members as to what they experienced.
30 min.	Discussion questions:

- Which of the four approaches was easiest for you? Which most difficult?
- Did you see any relationship between your spiritual style and the style of scripture reading you prefer? (see opening paragraphs of chapter 8).
- How do you think this approach to scripture reading might be useful to you?

Assign reading of chapter 6 for next session.
Dismiss

Session 4:
Making Decisions toward Growth

If your workshop is the four-session version, session 4 will be your last in the series. If you sense a strong interest, you might suggest that any who wish may continue with another four sessions as a way of going deeper into the study. It is preferable to have previously planned and announced the longer series. Anticipate losing about half the group if you make the second week optional.

In session 4 briefly summarize what has been done in the previous three meetings, with some discussion as to what was most valuable. It will also be important to put to use the insights gained by the inquiry.

If you're leading an eight-session workshop, omit the opening summary and give fifteen minutes to each of the three ten–minute discussion questions.

| 10 min. | Greetings, refreshments |
| 10 min. | Summarize what has been covered so far: |

- The circle and its axes.
- What was discovered in taking the selector test.
- The *lectio divina* experience in working with scripture.

So what do we do with what we have learned?

10 min.	Discussion about the *congregation:*
	• What is the consensus of this group about the nature of our congregation?
	• How would we describe ourselves to someone else?
10 min.	Discussion about the *congregation:*
	• In what ways are we different from other congregations in our community? The same?
10 min.	Discussion about *personal spirituality:*
	• What is the most important thing you have discovered about your own spirituality? (Include your own response.)
10 min.	Break
30 min.	Discussion about *making decisions for growth:*
	• What changes, if any, would you suggest to encourage growth in this congregation?
	• What changes, if any, have occurred to you as possibilities for enhancing your personal spiritual growth?
Dismiss	Refreshments if this is your last session.
	Those planning an eight-session workshop: Assign the reading of the chapter-2 section marked "Integration."

Study Guide for an Eight-Session Workshop

For sessions 1 through 4, follow the lesson outlines as they are given above. We suggest four sessions per week for two weeks, possibly Monday through Thursday, leaving the weekend free. The purpose of the second week is to go more deeply into a study of spiritual type and its implications for personal growth and to see its effect in history. Here we cover the material on integration, individuation, and on the life of Jesus as example. We include the interesting study done by Holmes that relates to periods of history that exhibit characteristics of spiritual type.

Session 5:
Integration—A Mark of Maturity

Carefully read the section marked "Integration," found in chapter 2. In your introduction include several dictionary definitions of *integration.*

　　Note that you are beginning the group again after three days of not meeting together. Consider including in session 5 the summary suggested in the outline for session 4. Session 4 will not suffer from leaving out the summary; you will then have more discussion time. The following outline for this session begins with the opening summary.

10 min.	Greetings, refreshments
15 min.	Review what has been covered so far.
	• The circle and its axes.
	• What was discovered in taking the Spirituality Wheel Selector?
	• The *lectio divina* experience in working with scripture.
	• Recommendations we made for congregation and for self.
10 min.	Introduce the word *integration.*
	• How is it used psychologically?
	• Has anyone ever known a person he would scribe as being integrated?
	What characteristics does that person have? Any comments on this person's religious life?

10 min.	Break
45 min.	Discuss any or all of the following questions. Rearrange them if you wish. As leader engage the members in discussion and guard against using your own personal reminiscences for anything but forwarding the discusion.

- Read aloud the quotation by Abraham Maslow (near the beginning of chapter 2), which describes the tendencies of organized religions. Is this true of any religious organizations you have observed? What effect has this had on society? What effect on you?
- Are there symbols or rituals in your religious life that have been transformed from mere formality into living, meaningful parts of your life? Examples: bread, wine, water.
- Do you recall your feelings when you were in your late teens? Did you suspect then that there was more than one "you"?
- Have the years caused any of these parts of yourself to come together more comfortably? Can you give an example of this integration within yourself?
- What values in your upbringing have you kept until today? What have you discarded? Why have you made these choices?
- What past values has our society maintained? What values have disintegrated? How has keeping or losing these values affected your life today?

Assign reading of "Individuation" section in chapter 2.
Dismiss

Session 6:
Individuation—A Second Mark of Maturity

Personal individuation is, in some ways, the flip side of integration. If all we do is integrate the past and harmonize the disparate parts of our inner selves, we have achieved only half of what we need. We may be peaceful but fail to be creative and growing. Look up the words *individuation* and *differentiation* to learn their use as terms in psychology. The following outline gives another series of discussion questions aimed at rounding out the dual concepts of integration and individuation.

10 min.	Greeting, refreshments
15 min.	Introduce the word *individuation* as the necessary complement to *integration,* studied during the last session. Let members say how these two word meanings differ.
10 min.	Ask if anyone has ever known a person she would describe as being individuated.

- What characteristics does that person have?
- Have you made observations about this person's religious life?

10 min.	Break
45 min.	Discuss any or all of the following questions. Rearrange them if you wish.

- Has it ever been necessary for you to separate yourself from family? From childhood faith beliefs? From community, state, or country? Which separation was the most difficult for you?
- If you have made any major changes in your life, how have you managed the anxiety of the separation or loss?
- Are there any major life-changes you feel you should have made and didn't? Are there any changes you believe you need to make to be true to yourself?
- What risks can you recall having taken? What risks has your faith community taken as a group?
- How do you view people who worship in a way different from yours? Do you ever visit their worship services?
- Do you feel you are more integrated than individuated? Neither? Both? On what do you base your assessment?

Assign the reading of the section marked "*Imitatio Christi*" in chapter 2. Dismiss

Session 7:
Jesus as a Model of Wholeness

The discussion of Jesus as a model of spiritual wholeness is based on the concepts of integration and individuation, explored in sessions 5 and 6. The term *wholeness* is popular in medicine, pastoral counseling, and mind–body work. In this study we want to show the creative *balance* present in Jesus' life: his ability to appreciate and use his heritage and his choice to risk being "different" within that context. Such a person is a model for wholeness of life, for realized potential, and for fulfilling one's highest destiny.

This outline, like those for sessions 5 and 6, is based on probing discussion questions. The purpose of the questions is not to bring members into theological agreement as to who Jesus is. That is a discussion for another time and occasion. These questions are designed to help us realize what we actually think about this person, sometimes unconsciously, and whether we wish to continue holding these images in our minds. When accepting a model, it is wise to be as accurate as possible about what that model is like. We know little about the historical Jesus, and what information we do have is under continual and lively debate. We do know some things, however, and will do well to be as realistic about those facts as we can. During this discussion some will not agree on what the "facts" are about Jesus. Focus the discussion on "what is Jesus like to *me*?" The following questions may help to uncover this very personal and important information.

10 min.	Greetings, refreshments
5 min.	Briefly review integration and individuation. We will now look at Jesus as a possible example of both.
15 min.	Discussion:

- Draw the circle on the board and ask the group members to comment on what about it reminds them of integration. Intersect the circle with the two lines, and ask what this says about individuation. Is it significant that the lines are inside the circle, or that the circle has been cut into parts?
- Looking at Jesus' life, do you see characteristics

of both integration and individuation? What about his life reveals this?

- Discuss the importance of models or "example people" in your own life. How do we learn to be a man or woman? A good person?

10 min.	Break
50 min.	Discuss any or all of the following questions. Rearrange them if you wish. The purpose of the first four questions is to reveal how much our imagination is colored by our culture, rather than by facts. The last four questions have to do with important personal experience.

- In your imagination, do you see Jesus as Jewish, or as a non-Jewish person living among Jews? Do you see him as resembling any Hollywood film figure? Book illustration? Painting? (Say what you actually imagine, not what you believe you should think.)

- In your thoughts of Jesus, what language do you imagine him to speak?

- Do you believe Jesus could see into the future? If so, how was he able to do that? (Refer to the prophetic section in chapter 2.) The group does not need to reach agreement. Discuss with the goal of discovering how you feel about Jesus' human-divine powers.

- What is the function of a prophet in society? Do you see anyone today whom you would think of as prophetic?

- Have you ever had what might be described as a "desert experience"? What, if any, was the lasting effect on you of this experience?

- What is it about Jesus that most moves you? Affects you?

- Do you typically think of Jesus as a rebel? A gentle person? A risk taker?

- What do you regard as Jesus' most important life choice?

Assign the reading of chapter 9.
Dismiss

Session 8:
Spirituality and History

If you are reading this book straight through in sequence, you have yet to read chapter 9 about spirituality and its connection to history. Holmes speculated that the typology he developed applies to periods of history, just as it does to groups and to individuals. It makes for a fascinating discussion and is an ideal way to end the series. Here a possible world view is added to the views we have developed so far about ourselves and our worshipping community.

Again, keep in mind that the purpose of this session is not to achieve agreement. These are ideas that involve history and also politics, and we can assume that there will be differences of opinion. The purpose of session 8 is to explore to its global limits the theory with which we have previously dealt. As the group facilitator, you do not need to be anxious about your own knowledge of history. You are the discussion leader, not the professor. Discussion questions will guide the group down a sequence of ideas, and you are there to see that things move along. As always, those who have read the chapter and thought about the questions it raises will be the most interested and will likely contribute most to the group.

The last set of discussion questions considers what we can learn from being "in tension" with the opposite quadrant of a type, and how we relate to the quadrants on each side of a type. These final questions are a way of bringing us back to the entire study of types and of thinking about ways we can grow spiritually from what we have learned.

Since this is the last part of an in-depth study, and participants have been dealing with material that has revealed inner feelings, there may be a camaraderie and unity among the members. You may want to create an opportunity for the group members to celebrate and say good–bye, at least for now. So that none will be forced to miss this time, allow at least twenty minutes before closing time to serve something special, such as a cake or pizza. Everyone can contribute to the pot, and nobody will need to bear the expense alone. You might recruit someone else to take care of these details for you, but make a place for this important celebration.

10 min.	Greetings, coffee
20 min.	What do members think about the whole idea of history

reflecting spiritual characteristics? Is Holmes stretching things, or is he accurate about the connections he makes? Review the ideas that Holmes puts forth.

- Sense of power, political predictability: speculative spirituality.
- Fewer boundaries and roles, less intellectual emphasis: affective spirituality.
- Security: kataphatic spirituality.
- Collapse of social institutions: apophatic spirituality.
- Loss of personal power, ill-defined roles: pietism.

10 min.   Break

30 min.   Discuss any or all of the following questions. Rearrange them if you wish.

- What do you consider to be the spirituality of the present time? Why do you think this is the case?
- Do you believe that you and your congregation reflect the times? What leads you to conclude that you do? Do not?
- What do you think could happen that would produce another type of spiritual expression in society? In you?

Questions to close the series:

- What is the value to you of learning about the quadrant opposite your primary spiritual characteristic? What is the benefit of keeping these two quadrants "in tension"? Does a congregation grow from maintaining this tension with the opposite (see chapter 3)?
- Do you feel that you have more difficulty relating to or accepting people who identify with the quadrants on either side of your primary quadrant? If so, why might this happen? Does this nonacceptance also creep into congregations?

20 min.   Dismiss and celebrate

Conclusion

One parting word. The workshop study is now concluded, and perhaps
your community has also participated in a congregation-wide survey.
Now, while there is a heightened interest in both personal and corporate
identity, be creative in "running with" what you've learned. The next
chapter, "Using Congregational Feedback to Plan for Growth," examines
just how you can put to use the corporate information you gather. Chapter 7, "Using the Wheel in Personal Growth and Spiritual Direction,"
addresses the personal and individual applications of what is discovered
about spiritual type. It is specifically for the reader interested in a personal spiritual journey or engaged in the spiritual companionship of
others. Whatever your pursuit, corporate or individual, *use what you
have learned.* Nothing is so counterproductive as to become enthusiastic, and then, for some reason, realize that nothing comes of it. The next
two chapters are designed to help you convert insights into action; to
grow from what you now know.

CHAPTER VI

Using Congregational Feedback to Plan for Growth

In this chapter and the next we will consider two kinds of congregational growth: growth in number of members and growth in depth of spiritual experience. Most congregations are interested in numerical growth and a corresponding growth in revenues that support the community's efforts. This interest is not inevitably crass or irreverent; it is not the lesser of the two kinds of growth. Numerical growth is practical, to say the least, and can be ethical, even holy, if the motivations are focused on making life better for the people enlisted. If it is growth for the sake of validating the group or promoting the career of the leader, it is deadly.

Growth in the spiritual sense is usually a lesser concern, but, for the health of the community, it should be the priority. Too often we see congregations that begin in a fervor of faith grow large and then evolve into institutions primarily interested in perpetuating themselves. To borrow from Elton Trueblood's simile, they are like blooming flowers whose stems are cut, and no one has yet noticed that they are dying. The nourishment that sustains the congregation is its experience of growing faith and its connection with God; in other words, its *spirituality*. This is why we address in these chapters individual spiritual growth as well as corporate growth. The community is a fabric made of its individual members, and it is these people who nourish the community and provide both numerical and spiritual growth.

"Reading" the Data

Let's assume that you have met with the congregation at large, explained the Spirituality Wheel Selector test, and led them in filling it out. Someone has collected the tests and you are now faced with the challenge of how best to use this information. Within two weeks, while it is still on their minds, you will want to say something to the congregation about its profile or portrait and make comments on what this means for identity and for the future.

To help with corporate scoring, it will be helpful if test-takers have tallied the number of wheel spokes they have placed in each quadrant. They could write that number just outside the perimeter of the circle. It might look something like this.

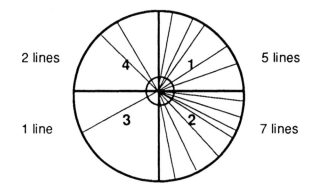

2 lines   5 lines

1 line   7 lines

Step 1

Gather the congregation's completed tests. Separate the tests into four stacks, one for each spirituality type. On each test determine which quadrant has the highest number of spokes in the bottom "personal style" circle. Place the test in the stack representing the tester's predominant type. (Make separate stacks of any that have first and second choices tied. Distribute them equally between the first and second choices.) When all the tests are in one of the four stacks, determine which stack contains the most tests. Write this information down. This first bit of information will tell you the predominate spiritual type of your congregation.

Step 2

To determine the second-rated strength of the group, gather the tests into a pile and start over; go through the process again, placing the tests in four piles determined by the second-highest number of spokes. This will tell you the second-strongest tendency of the congregation.

Step 3

Go through the process a third time, making piles based on the lowest number of spokes on the wheels. This will give you the least prominent spiritual type of this congregation.

Step 4

Using the information gathered in step 1 (predominant type) and the circle drawing on the following page, make a portrait of the congregation as a whole. It may be physically impossible to represent one person with one spoke. Place into the congregational profile wheel *one spoke for each unit of people*.

For congregations of

250 or fewer people	one spoke for every 10 people
250 to 500 people	one spoke for every 20 people
500 to 750 people	one spoke for every 30 people
750 to 1,000 people	one spoke for every 40 people

(continue to increase by increments of 250 members)

This congregational profile will be less accurate than the number amounts you gathered, but it will provide the congregation a visual and memorable way of seeing the whole congregational picture.

Our Congregational Profile

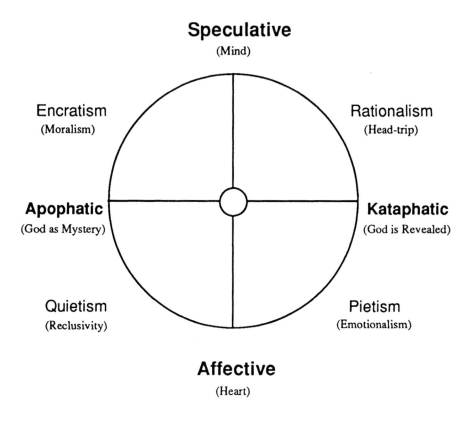

Speculative
(Mind)

Encratism
(Moralism)

Rationalism
(Head-trip)

Apophatic
(God as Mystery)

Kataphatic
(God is Revealed)

Quietism
(Reclusivity)

Pietism
(Emotionalism)

Affective
(Heart)

For congregations of 250 or less	one spoke for every 10 persons
For congregations of 250-500	one spoke for every 20 persons
For congregations of 500-750	one spoke for every 30 persons
For congregations of 750-1000	one spoke for every 40 persons

Adapted from *A History of Christian Spirituality* by Urban Holmes, III, p. 4, Copyright © 1980 by Urban Holmes, III. Reprinted by permission of Jane Holmes, Executrix.

Step 5

At this point you can do some interpretation for members. Here are some observations to consider in light of what you have learned from the test data.

1. "Our congregation's greatest strength is in its ability to . . . " Emphasize the gifts this group of people offers: intellectual gifts, feeling and warmth, deep prayer and inner strength, or a strong social conscience. Elaborate on what is good about the congregation. Mention what happens if we go overboard and do not achieve some appreciation and development in other areas (see chapter 3).

2. Cite the group's second-strongest tendency, emphasizing the gifts this brings to the membership and to the larger community. "We are also very good at . . . "

3. "The area in which we seem to have little experience is . . ." What does this mean for us? Below, under "What We Cannot Be," we will discuss the fact that congregations cannot "be everything." It is not possible to shine in all areas. One must choose paths of growth and ministry and not become trapped in the competition to become what another group is.

4. The area of greatest growth potential for the congregation is found in the quadrant opposite the group's primary tendency. This opposite quadrant encourages us to see the value of experiencing God in another way. We do not need to abandon our primary way of doing things. Indeed we would be foolish to try, since it cannot be done. But we can *stretch*. We will discuss below different ways to encourage growth toward new experience and ways to care for and enlist group members who differ from the majority.

5. Those in quadrants to either side of us are often the ones whom we least accept. We may or may not wish to do things as they do, but we can notice their contribution to the whole. It may be revealing to ask if some members feel a little irritation with a certain type of spirituality. Does the type-1 intellectual look down on the less heady, more emotional type 2? Does the type 2 belittle graduate education as "ruining your faith"?

Analyzing What You Know

Learning can be both negative and positive; we can learn as much from our failings as from what works for us. As you analyze the information from this study, it will be just as important to see what you do *not* need to be doing as it is to stretch toward your growing edge. The goal is not the establishment of a generic faith or of the Homogenized Church Universal. The goal for groups is the same as for individual people: to become individuated and distinctive, all the while integrating that which fosters growth.

What We Cannot Be

You'll want to assess whether your congregation is fairly typical of the larger organizational or faith group of which it is a part. Is what you learned from the test congruent with what you know of the larger group? You may find that you are not in favor of altering the established group characteristics or identity.

Imagine a local Episcopal church deciding that it will no longer conduct its worship services using the *Book of Common Prayer*. Instead, someone will decide from Sunday to Sunday what the service will contain, which scriptures will be used, and how the order of things will go. That is a perfectly good way to conduct things but any Episcopalian will tell you that a church that decides to discard the *BCP* will no longer *be* an Episcopal church. Each faith group has its character and flavor. It is marked by choices made by others in the past and agreed to by subsequent generations. If your faith group is characterized by a distinctive spirituality, there are reasons behind that distinction; you will want to consider seriously whether that spirituality has value for you. Different faith groups exist because they bring choice to the mix. At some time in the past someone wanted and perhaps fought for an alternative to the status quo, and that legacy is what you now have. It is possible, even desirable, that faith groups should change to reflect growth and new insight or to respond to outside need. Such changes are serious and should be carefully thought out.

You'll also want to assess your findings in light of your congregational mission. What does this group regard as its primary task? Is there something in particular, such as a social concern or a provided service, in which this group takes particular responsibility? If the group sees its mission as the preservation of religious truth through the maintenance of liturgy, it will never be successful with the informal, off-the-cuff style of worship as its main worship expression. If its primary mission is to invest energies in a soup kitchen and minister to the homeless in a downtown neighborhood, it is not likely to stop everything just to write a position paper or attend symposia. The liturgical group may, however, institute a casual Wednesday evening service that is secondary to the more formal main worship service. The soup kitchen brigade may consider a prayer and study group to fuel its spiritual side and prevent burnout in its often thankless labors. This is what is meant by *stretching*—determining the central, core identity and then deciding to move on to enhance and enlarge the spiritual tent.

We cannot be everything. That is why there are many of us. There is no reason to look at your congregational wheel portrait and lament that you are not strongly represented in each segment. But you can learn your areas of strength and then look for ways to appreciate and supplement experience. We are not engaged in a competition but a journey.

Positive Steps toward Growth

Once we have identified the area of our strength—that is, the spirituality we most favor when we worship or pray—we can consider new ideas and encounters. Here we can consider the concerns of people within the group who are different in their spirituality from the predominant group. For example, in a congregation that is 85 percent kataphatic (within one of the two quadrants to the right side of the circle), 15 percent are apophatics who see God as mystery and are somewhat contemplative. The needs of the 85 percent are probably being met. But what of the spiritual hungers of this 15 percent—a significant number? You may already have lost some of them, or you may want now to attend to them by providing some supplemental avenues for their worship experience. You will not be overhauling the entire church or temple program to do that, just enriching it with opportunities for small-group participation. In this way each person's spirituality is validated by the group; each is seen as valuable to the whole.

Here are only a very few suggestions as to how a congregation can enrich its worship expression to include more of its members. If we have learned anything from the study so far, it is that we should not expect all members to participate in all activities. Participation in activities is not a test of faith. The contemplative mystic who prays in her closet but does not attend potlucks is busy and equally faithful.

To read the following, think in terms of this statement: "If I wanted to strengthen a particular type of spirituality, I might try . . . "

Type 1. To strengthen the speculative-kataphatic:

1. Form study and discussion groups around the interests of members, using books, periodicals, tapes. Explore new publishing houses and authors. You can always choose to reject an undesirable idea.

2. Create a library for group use.

3. Begin a Bible-study group that will use concordances, Bible dictionaries, various scripture translations, and study helps.

4. Read chapter 8, *"Lectio Divina,"* and study on your own or as a group. Actually, this is an ideal activity for all four types.

5. Inform yourself by visiting other worship services. Invite guest speakers from various groups. Your goal is appreciation, not agreement.

Type 2. To strengthen the affective–kataphatic:

1. Experiment with musical expression. Have an informal service using only praise music and instruments other than the organ. You might schedule this on a weekday.

2. Arrange a time for people briefly to tell their faith stories to the group—how they were introduced to their faith, how it has affected their life, and how it has influenced recent events.

3. Occasionally leave the pulpit or lectern to deliver the sermon; speak at floor level, near the people.

4. "Dinner on the ground"—picnicking—is part of the American evangelical heritage, but anyone can do it. There is something warm and "type 2" about food and eating together outdoors.

5. If members often retreat to the lake or the mountains over the weekend, consider a casual Sunday evening service where T-shirts, sports gear, and tennis shoes are expected. You will attract an odd crew, but these services can be very peaceful and deeply moving.

Type 3. To strengthen the affective-apophatic:

1. Consider ways to include silence in the worship service. We are not trained to enjoy "no noise." For type 3, the yearning for it is often like a thirst. Just a little will help.

2. Form a group that gathers together and prays silently at a particular time for the worship service. Some type-3 people are so private they will not do this. That's fine. Ask them to pray privately for the service.

3. If you design a retreat for type-1 or type-2 members, you will want to plan group activities, a speaker, and program. For type 3, this only interferes. Consider providing a "director" to lead in meditation, read some short but powerful quotations, and direct periods of silence. Quiet, tonal music is an asset, as are crafts, reading, journaling, and walking in the woods.

4. Invite a leader to discuss with type 3 various ways to structure short prayers and meditations into a daily work life. This used to be called a "rule," and it is an effective and disciplined way to live.

5. For a variation on the daily rule, institute a corporate noontime prayer. Ask any who are interested to pray a silent, extemporaneous prayer or one chosen by the group. This is particularly significant to the group if all are joined in doing this at the same moment.

6. During a worship service, ask the congregation to read from the Psalms antiphonally. (Have two groups alternate in reading subsequent phrases or verses). The rhythmic quality to such reading nourishes the meditative temperament.

Type 4. To strengthen the speculative-apophatic:

While type 3 is a *being* person with vision, type 4 is a *doing* visionary. You may find few in your congregation who are dominant in this category. You may find more for whom this is a tendency but not predominant. Some have left the organized church for what they regard as ministry. The key type-4 words are a *cause*, a *mission*, and a meaningful *project*. All members, not only type 4, will grow from engaging in an effort that has human significance.

1. Habitat for Humanity has the flavor of a significant cause. So do other programs that provide food, work in the field of ecology, and fight for moral issues within the political process. Inasmuch as your congregation will take a stand on these matters, you will keep, even attract, a type-4 spirituality.

2. For some congregations, the Stephen Ministries lay training program is a good avenue for significant service.[1]

3. Less dramatic, but also effective, are local efforts to provide services to the elderly, the housebound, and day care for children. Some might enjoy work with what is often called the "building and grounds" committee. When the floods of 1993 wiped out the town of Elwood, Missouri, local congregations joined together with a group from Texas; they cleaned out the water and mud from the homes of several elderly residents who had been stranded. This is the sort of significant action that appeals to people who like to say, "My work is my prayer."

Of course there are dozens of other things that can be adapted to enrich your worship community. Take your time. Consider your options. Change bothers people. It also "grows" them.

CHAPTER VII

Using the Wheel in Personal Growth and Spiritual Direction

Chapter 6 addressed readers interested in applying the principles of spiritual type to an analysis of congregational spirituality. Understanding individual spirituality, however, is as essential to church leaders as it is to those seeking personal growth. This chapter is for the reader looking for that individual insight. It is also for the person who accompanies others in what is commonly called spiritual direction. As I have said earlier, I do not care for the term *director*, but prefer *companion* or *guide*. *Direction* and *director* are traditionally used but are not necessarily descriptive of what takes place.

The Wheel and Individual Direction

I originally developed the Spirituality Wheel Selector test for use in individual spiritual direction; it is the result of my work on the staff of a pastoral counseling center that provides spiritual formation services. In addition to my role as psychotherapist, I am the staff member who directs the center's spiritual formation services. Though there are many spiritual assessment instruments, most are focused on client history and opinion, attempting to show a level of maturity in spiritual development. What I wanted was something different; something indicating type rather than ranking maturity or stages of faith.

As a spiritual director, I have noticed that each person exhibits very pronounced and different religious needs. This often has seemingly nothing to do with "maturity"; rather, it has to do with an inner-directed and innate spiritual temperament. I felt I needed an instrument that would give the insight into spiritual type that is similar to what is evidenced

about personal temperament by the Myers-Briggs Type Indicator test
(MBTI). I still do give the MBTI to people beginning in spiritual
direction. Myers has written a book called *Gifts Differing* which I highly
recommend to spiritual directors.[1]

When I saw Urban Holmes's book *A History of Christian Spirituality*, I realized that the typology for spiritual type was there. But how was
I to put it into practical application with clients? Using the typology
ideas in interviews with clients, I saw that people frequently have several
kinds of spiritual tendency, not just one. Holmes said this himself. I developed the Spirituality Wheel Selector test so as to reflect all of a person's preferences, not just one, as would be done by a forced-choice test.
The result is a "portrait" of one's spirituality at the time the test is taken.

What You Can Learn about Yourself

After taking the test the first thing you notice is that you *do* have a type
of spirituality. You may have wondered what was wrong with you or
whether you were spiritual enough when you were uncomfortable with
some of the rituals, or lack of them, in your worship setting. Or you may
have wondered why some people are so focused on activities while
others seems to find their spiritual nourishment in silent retreats. Everyone, including you, has a capacity for the spiritual—but that spiritual
capacity expresses itself in a variety of ways.

In looking at your wheel profile, note that your tendencies probably
are not located in just one quadrant of the circle. (If it is, return to chapter 4 and read about the four types and what an exclusively narrow focus
in any one type may indicate.) Looking at your spoked wheel, you can
identify your predominant strength and see where your other capabilities
show up. Knowing your chief tendency will help you understand that
what and who you are is *just fine*. You do not need to have the same
desires as others. The Creator has made you to find your connection to
the Holy in a particular way. Our spiritual formation comes from both
nature and nurture; temperament and environment.

But the test-picture also tells you that to grow, to expand your
spiritual capacity, you would do well to explore the quadrant opposite
your predominant type. Also look to each side of your predominant
quadrant. Do you find that these are the people to whom you sometimes

object, with whom you are sometimes impatient? It helps to know what is likely to get under your skin.

If you have taken the test using both wheels, you have in front of you a picture of your personal spiritual picture as compared to your congregation's portrait. I have a friend who finally understood his life-long discontent when he saw that his own spirituality wheel was a mirror image of his church's spirituality; they were exactly opposite. He has strong family ties that encourage him to remain where he is, but at last he under-stands that he is not an uncooperative or poor member, just one who must nourish his spiritual side in additional ways that are suited to his nature.

Making a Plan to Nourish Needs

Whether you are on an individual journey or are a person interested in the art of spiritual guidance, formal or informal, you can use the information about spiritual type to be more sensitive in planning paths for growth. In doing so, consider both the strength of your predominant type and the growing edge presented by its opposite. There is an explanation of the four spiritual types introduced in chapter 3. The following treatment of the four types is similiar but directed more to personal growth.

Type 1:
Speculative-Kataphatic—A Head Spirituality

Predominance in this quadrant is demonstrated in a love of order and a desire for things to be logical and consistent. You have probably found your high spiritual moments in hearing something said that stirred you to a moment of understanding or in reading a passage that seemed to say exactly what you felt to be true. You may find very appealing the idea of an orderly and perfect creation—of "all things working together." The Jewish ideal of study-as-worship has descendants in many Christian churches of the speculative-kataphatic type.

Note that there must be no effort to discover one's predominant tendency only to obliterate it for another tendency. The way you naturally find God and the way you most often experience high moments are your surest access to the deepest part of yourself. If the written word has power for you, cooperate with your strength and set out on a very intentional reading program. Get the help of someone whose scholarship you trust and ask that person to guide you as you get started. If a particular book has significantly changed your life, look at its bibliography and follow the trail, so to speak, of that line of thought. Subscribe to periodicals and journals that speak to your main interest. For many, reading would be the last way in the world to become spiritual. But for people who love words and ideas, *reading is the avenue of God's speech.* As example, almost every congregation of any size includes a person or two who is studying Hebrew or Greek. These people want to read in the original biblical languages to feed their sense of God speaking to them through the meaning of words.

Many in type 1 are attracted to good public speakers who can make an interesting and congruent presentation of ideas. Especially appreciated by type 1 is the person who can lead in the study of scripture. Avail yourself of the many opportunities to hear new ideas and to visit groups that invite knowledgeable speakers. Type 1 is not as inclined as most to swallow everything presented. Cultivate an open mind but retain the critical faculty as well.

If there is little balance in life, a type 1 can become "dry" and out of touch with real-life feelings. Sometimes this type is described as being on a "head trip." This usually implies an emotional tone is missing; what Holmes referred to as the *affective* has been suppressed. This is why developing the other aspects of spiritual expression is so important. Type 1 may detest unthinking emotionalism occasionally seen in type-2 behavior and in reaction feel there is reason not to "give in to feelings." But type-2 expression of feelings need not be without discernment. It can be as informed and careful of credibility as the scholarship so admired by type 1. It is important for type 1 to appreciate that a capacity for emotional responsiveness does not necessarily equate with gullibility.

The growing edge for type 1 is the more mystic experience of its opposite quadrant, in which the intellectual faculty must suspend itself and practice a sort of waiting before God. Here there is no need to ask what, exactly, is being said to you by God, or whether God is or is not speaking. The object is quietly to *enjoy* God—to be in God's presence as an end in itself. A type 1 may strongly feel that there is no point to this sort of thing. What have you learned from "doing nothing"? you may ask. Just consider the possibility that there is more than one way to know a thing or a person. We can learn facts about something, and we can also know that thing or person by simply "being with." You can acknowledge that this is not now a strength for you. But your predominant tendency need not prevent you from understanding what the type-3 experience is about. Occasionally we discover that we have a latent capability that has been as yet untapped because of our cultural and educational formation. This is especially true for type 1. By exploring our opposite quadrant, we can often discover a new frontier within ourselves.

Type 2:
Affective-Kataphatic—A Heart Spirituality

A person who is predominantly type 2 may experience highs and lows in religious feeling. The high moments are uplifting, even extraordinary and memorable. The low points may be worrisome, even depressing. The speculative half of the circle, types 1 and 4, may look with envy at the capacity of type 2 to experience high moments with such intensity. They may look at an active, growing, predominantly type-2 congregation and say, "If we just sing the same songs, have speakers with more 'fire,' and cultivate a less-structured atmosphere, we too will feel all these things; our congregation will also grow by leaps and bounds." One reason such congregations are growing so rapidly at this time is that the society as a whole thirsts for experiences that will move us to emotion. Life in a technological and impersonal environment can leave us with a yearning for relationship and meaning.

The strength of type 2 is in the richness of feeling. Their great gift is their ability to experience God in the moment, to revel in what is happening around them, to be in the present tense. But they need to remember that God has not departed just because one moment is not as high as a previous moment. God is consistently "there." Accept and enjoy the way you are in your spirituality. Value the low points along with the peak moments; they furnish context and contrast to the more ecstatic times, making them all the more precious.

Since so much of type-2 spirituality is affected by circumstance— the here and now moment—you will want to see that you are fed by the experiences that promote your feelings of connection to God. Seek out places where a warm and informal worship style is used, where the music lifts you. A regular, weekly meeting with others whose spiritual expression suits yours is important for keeping up your spirits. You may enjoy playing tapes of religious music while in the car or when working at home.

You will want to guard against the assumption that to be "right" everyone else must share a spiritual experience similar to yours. Wonderful as your way is for you, it is not the only way. You may be tempted to view type 1 as having missed the boat spiritually; you may assume that too much learning has ruined what was once (or what could be) a perfectly good faith. You may see the more mystical type 3 as being out of touch with the spiritual realities that you know about. Being defensive or exclusive will not help you to grow or cause you to appreciate the variety of spiritual expression around you. Try to avoid the smugness of thinking that your way is the only true and legitimate way of thinking about God. Because of your deep feelings, you are capable of persuading and influencing others. You will want to be careful with that power.

Growing toward your opposite quadrant might be very beneficial, once you accept as God-given your own spiritual strengths as well as those of others. Your opposite, type 4, is the visionary who thinks critically. You might feel challenged to put some of your enthusiasm to work on behalf of a social cause that will benefit many people—beyond your own group. Like type 4, you might decide to research that cause to learn the facts about it, rather than taking the word of others as to whether or not it is worthwhile. Two qualities that can be gained from your opposite type-4 quadrant are a broad rather than a local consciousness and a critical thinking that helps prevent one from misjudging the issues.

Type 3:
Affective-Apophatic—A Mystic Spirituality

I have often called this type the "questers" because these people seem to be perpetually on a *journey*. In fact *journey* is one of their favorite words. The myths about the search for the Holy Grail make perfect sense to the type 3. They never reach the destination, of course, but it is the journey that matters. The great gift of type 3 is the ability to penetrate past the temporal, past what is physically seen and heard, and to engage in a "deeper sort of knowing." For this type, *being* is more important than *doing*, because the doing will pass away. When you meet a type 3 whose spirituality is well developed, you may feel as if you are at the eye of the storm where all is calm within the chaos. The type 3 who has not given much attention to her spiritual life may feel very restless, often because she is aware of the "more" for which she yearns but has not spent time or energy to pursue.

If you think about it, most of the inspirational books that "change lives" are by affective-apophatic writers. This type reminds us that there is more to life than just "stuff." There is a reality, they say, that transcends what can be named and measured. At this point in history, there is a resurgence of this sort of spirituality and an appreciation of the transcendent reality it represents. Thomas Moore's book *Care of the Soul* was on the best-seller lists longer than anyone could have imagined. We may or may not agree with the spirituality promoted by actress Shirley MacLaine, but we cannot deny the enormous readership of her books.

The yearning for the inner life is on the rise, and, though you may choose other writers, it is the type 3 who can guide in understanding the riches available through cultivating this spirituality.

To grow, a type 3 needs inner silence in which to make a closer connection with God. The Desert Fathers and Mothers did not move to the desert primarily to punish or deprive themselves, but to live without distraction so that they could more fully focus their attention on God. If this is where you find your predominant tendency, my guess is that you are drawn to techniques of meditation and contemplation. When you enjoy music, it is probably the sort that evokes the mysterious and fosters interior reflection. When you go on a spiritual retreat, your favorite part may be walking alone in the woods or sitting quietly with a trusted friend. You may enjoy sharing your experience with others, but you do so on your terms, which means in a deeply personal, one-on-one way. Especially in a society that places such a premium on being "outgoing," it may be hard for you to remember that a desire for silence does not necessarily indicate a lack of social development, nor is it an indication that you just don't like people. Take yourself seriously. You have a legitimate and valuable type of spirituality. Feed yourself with time alone, with poetry and meditation, with wordless prayer and with the enjoyment of rocks, trees, candles, art, books, and all the other things that move you to consider God with gladness.

Without a balancing tension, the type 3 might retreat from life in a way that is too reclusive. Admittedly, a few people are called to a life of physical solitude—to a vocation of unselfish retreat dedicated to prayer for the world and its needs. Most people, however, are invited by God to interact with the world by being physically and emotionally present to others. The affective-apophatic person will want to guard against becoming so self-absorbed or so self-protective that only his life (and relationship with God) holds his interest. One of the characteristics of a developed spiritual life is its *inclusiveness*.

Type 3 may have some difficulty with the types on either side. Type 2 may seem abrasively superficial and outer-determined. Type 3 may wish that type 4 were less driven.

Again, the growing edge is the opposite quadrant. Type 1 can teach type 3 to ask, "Does this make sense?" and, "Is this realistic and logical?" The thinking-and-touching type can give type 3 a beneficial "reality check" and grounding.

Type 4:
Speculative-Apophatic—A Kingdom Spirituality

As we have pointed out, the type 4 is probably the least represented in the general population, certainly within worshipping congregations. Often the roots of their social concerns come out of the church or synagogue in which they grew up. They have been known to leave those congregations, however, because they become impatient with the perceived lack of concern. By promoting their visions and insisting that others join in, they can be disruptive to settled-in congregations. Of course, if the congregation buys into the vision, the type 4 can become a heroic leader seen as an agent for change.

If your predominant tendency is in the type-4 quadrant, try to find a hospitable, like-minded community that shares your vision. It doesn't have to be large. It could be the staff of a publication, a political group, Habitat for Humanity folks, or people who meet and organize a "walk on hunger." When you feel great intensity about a certain cause, you need the support of others to keep you from burning out or becoming bitter. When interest in your cause is not widely shared, you must intentionally look for that support.

Because you value the intellectual side of things, furnish yourself with the cognitive stimulation that "makes your motor run." Seek out people who have original ideas and write on the subjects that interest you. You may be tempted to become so involved with your cause or project that you neglect the interior reflection that means so much to you. See to it that you attend as much to the inner life as to the outer life. One will nourish the other; your great strength is that you are able to keep one foot in each.

It is probably not difficult for you to see what can happen if you lack balance in your life created by the tension of other influences. Others may have told you that you have a one-track mind, or that you have no patience with people who do not share your vision. Your great gift to others is that you do offer judgment and cause us to be more responsible. If it goes too far, however, it can be wounding and can lose you the support you need. If you want to get things done, you may need to look at the rest of us with appreciation and gratitude, as well as with judgment.

In your impatient moments, you may be intensely irritated with the quadrants to each side of you. In your eyes, type 1 may talk a good game but not accomplish anything of substance; type 3 has its head in the clouds and is good for little. This analysis might be true, but do not fail to notice that each spirituality type has its own gift—and you are the recipient of some of those gifts. Your passion, after all, did not begin with you. Someone lit the fire.

What nourishment for growth does type 2, the opposite quadrant, offer you? The deeper religious feelings that you may have neglected. Type 2 demonstrates the enjoyment of spirituality and may save you from a certain grimness. Type-2 qualities may bring you down to earth, so to speak, and persuade you to think of God as being in the present world as well as in that future for which you hope. The world needs you badly. Take care of yourself and nourish the spirituality that so effectively demonstrates itself in effecting societal change.

Combinations of Types

The portrait of your spirituality probably reveals your predominant tendency and a strong second preference. You may even have spokes in a third and perhaps fourth quadrant. This is all to the good. Count yourself fortunate if you show some balance among the quadrants. This provides a healthy tension that will enrich your connection with God and your appreciation of others.

Everyone will have one way of doing things that seems most natural. Your long-term goal is not to draw a wheel that has an equal number of spokes in each of the quadrants. By understanding where you are now, you can see to it that what serves you best is not neglected, while being challenged to develop new ways of experiencing the Holy. If you wish to gain more insight into how people of other types exercise their spirituality, talk to them. See what is most important to them and then participate in as much of that with them as you can. By exploring new ways of experiencing God, you will not necessarily be trying to be something you are not or trying to change congregational allegiance. You can see this as venturing into new territory so as to increase worship options available to you.

Many readers will wonder if this experimentation with spiritual experience is dangerous. What if we believe something that is not true or take up a practice that harms our spiritual connection with God?

Well, that is a possibility to consider before you experiment. Ask yourself just what it is that could be harmful about what you are about to experience. Afterward, see if you feel closer to God or further from God as a result of the experience. Notice what those around you are like. Does their form of worship make of their lives something that you admire? If you don't like what it does to them, consider trying to understand what is going on, even if you do not choose to imitate their expressions of spirituality.

God is not fragile nor does God do things in only one way. The essence of creativity is variety, and God is certainly creative. Although we do not want to endanger ourselves, we may be certain that experiencing God in new ways will not destroy us. There is a certain stewardship of self in allowing God to speak in other voices.

Suggestions for Individual Meditation

Chapter 5 presented three plans for leading a workshop on the Spirituality Wheel Selector test and its ideas. One plan is a one-day presentation, another is a one-week workshop, and the third extends that week into a two-week study. The meditations below are loosely based on the in-depth questions given in the second week of the two-week study.

As presented in chapter 5, the in-depth questions are for group discussion, which by its nature presents time restrictions. Working individually, allow yourself much longer to consider the questions presented below, perhaps as long as a day or a week for each question. I strongly suggest that you write something down. Jot down a few thoughts about each question, or write more fully in a journal. There is something about writing on paper that validates our thoughts and causes us to take them seriously. I also recommend that you review these questions and your journal annually as a way to track what has happened to you over a year's time.

Questions for Meditation

Meditations on Integration as a Mark of Maturity

Carefully read again the section marked "Integration" in chapter 2. Read especially the definition and how the word is used psychologically.

1. Have you ever known anyone you would describe as being integrated? What characteristics does that person have? Do you have any thoughts or observations about this person's religious life?

2. Read again the quotation by Abraham Maslow (near the beginning of chapter 2), which describes the tendencies of organized religions. Is this true of any religious organizations you have observed? What effect has this had on society? What effect on you?

3. Are there symbols or rituals in your religious life that have been transformed from mere formality into living, meaningful parts of your life? Examples: bread, wine, water.

4. Try to go back and re-create your feelings when you were in your late teens. Did you suspect then that there was more than one "you"?

5. Have the years caused any of these parts of yourself to come together more comfortably? Have you noticed that your attitudes toward yourself and others have changed? Can you think of an example of this integration within yourself? Within the last year?

6.   What values in your upbringing have you kept until today? What have you discarded? Why have you made these choices?

7.   What past values has our society maintained? What values have disintegrated? How has keeping or losing these values affected your life today?

Meditations on Individuation as a Second Mark of Maturity

Personal individuation is, in some ways, the flip side of integration. If we successfully integrate the past and harmonize the disparate parts of our inner selves, we have achieved only half of what we need. We may be peaceful but fail to be creative—living out the potential of all we're meant to be.

Look up the words *individuation* and *differentiation* to learn their use as terms in psychology. The following questions are designed to round out your reflections on the dual concepts of integration and individuation as experienced in your life.

1.   Have you ever known a person you would describe as being individuated? Imagine that person now. What particular characteristics does that person have? Can you recall anything about that person's religious life?

2.   Has it ever been necessary for you to separate yourself from your family? From childhood faith beliefs? From community, state, or country? Describe your feelings before, during, and after the separation.

3.   If you have experienced any major changes in your life, how did you manage the anxiety of that separation or loss?

4.   Are there any major life-changes you feel you should have made in your life and didn't? Are there any changes you need to make now to be true to yourself? Consider this carefully.

5.   What risks can you recall having taken? What risks has your faith community taken as a group?

6.   How do you view people who worship in a way different from yours? Have you ever visited their worship services? How would you feel about such a visit?

7.   Do you feel that you are more integrated than individuated? Neither? Both? On what do you base your assessment?

Meditations on Jesus as a Model of Wholeness

Our consideration of Jesus as a model of a full spiritual life is based on the concepts of integration and individuation explored in previous meditations and in chapter 2. The term *wholeness* is popular now in medicine, pastoral counseling, and mind-body work. Here let's consider the creative *balance* present in Jesus' life: his ability to appreciate and use his heritage, along with his choice to risk being "different" within that context. Such a person is a model for wholeness of life, for realized potential, and for fulfilling one's highest destiny.

The purpose of these questions is not to bring you into theological agreement with anyone else as to who Jesus is. Rather, the questions are designed to help you realize what you actually think about this person, sometimes unconsciously, and whether you wish to continue holding these images in your mind. When accepting a model, it is wise to be as accurate as possible about what that model is like. We know little about the historical Jesus, and what we do have is under continual debate. We do know some things, however, and will do well to be as realistic about these facts as we can. During this meditation the important question is "What is Jesus like to *me*?" The following questions may help you uncover this very personal and important information.

Questions 1 and 2 are to help you meditate on the person of Jesus as a model for your own life. The purpose of questions 3 through 6 is to reveal how much our imagination is colored by our own culture, rather than by facts and by reality. Questions 7 through 10 have to do with important personal experience.

1. Looking at Jesus' life, do you see characteristics of both integration and individuation? What about his life reveals this? (You may need to look again at the circle and its intersecting lines.)

2. Think about the importance of models or "example people" in your own life. From whom did you learn to be a man or woman? A "good person"?

3. In your imagination, do you see Jesus as Jewish, or as a non-Jewish person living among Jews? Do you see him as resembling any Hollywood film figure? Book illustration? Painting? (Respond with what you actually imagine, not what you believe you should think.)

4. In your thoughts of Jesus, what language do you imagine him to be speaking?

5.   Do you believe that Jesus could see into the future? If so, how was he able to do that? (Refer to the prophetic section in chapter 2.) Reflect with the goal of discovering how you feel about Jesus' human-divine powers.

6.   What do you see as the function of a prophet in society? Do you see anyone today you would think of as prophetic?

7.   Have you ever had what is thought of as a "desert experience"? What, if any, was the experience's lasting effect on you?

8.   What is it about Jesus that most moves you? Affects you?

9.   Do you typically think of Jesus as a rebel? As a gentle person? As a risk taker? Why do you think of him in this way?

10. What do you think was Jesus' most important life choice?

Reflections on Spirituality and History

If you are reading this book straight through in sequence, you have yet to read the chapter about spirituality and its connection to history. Holmes speculated that the typology he developed applies to periods of history just as it does to groups and to individual people. After reading chapter 9, return to the following questions for further reflection on spirituality and its connection to history. It makes for a fascinating study; it is an ideal way to deepen your meditation. It also helps to open up a wider world view, one of the goals of spiritual meditation.

1. What do you think about the whole idea of history reflecting spiritual characteristics? Is Holmes stretching things?

2. How would you categorize the spirituality of the present time? Why do you feel this is the case?

3. Do you feel as if your spirituality "reflects the times"? What makes you think you do? Do not? Does your worshipping congregation reflect the times? Are you pleased or bothered by that?

4. Try to imagine what could happen nationally or globally that would produce another type of spiritual expression in society. Try to imagine what could happen that would produce another type of spiritual expression in you.

Pathways toward Growth

These two concluding questions consider what we can learn from being "in tension" with the opposite quadrant of our predominant type and how we can relate to the quadrants on each side of our type. This study is not complete without a meditation on how to prepare for growth.

1. What will be the personal benefits or value to you of keeping your dominant and opposite quadrants "in tension"?

2. Do you have more difficulty relating to or accepting people who are temperamentally in the quadrants on either side of your primary quadrant? If so, why do you think this happens?

The words *tension* and *balance* lead one to think about *wholeness.* Though we cannot force spiritual moments, we can clear a path for them. As a result of such epiphanies, we become more nearly who we were designed to be; we move toward being whole rather than partially developed people.

CHAPTER VIII

Lectio Divina

This chapter presents an exercise that draws on the strengths of all four spirituality types to accomplish a single thing: to more deeply read and pray the scriptures. There is joy in engaging in each type of spirituality, realizing that your capability is greater than you had thought.

Lectio divina, first used in the fourth and fifth centuries, is a highly effective method of praying with scripture. The two Latin words mean "sacred reading." It is a remarkable way of experiencing a scripture passage in the four ways we have studied. This method is excellent for those who want to enrich their personal meditation time or for those who need to prepare sermons and lessons on a particular passage. It is especially helpful if you know you will be asked to comment on some passage that does not as yet inspire you. The approach has been associated with the Benedictine orders and seems to have originated with the Eastern Desert Fathers, particularly John Cassian. Today Benedictine and Cistercian orders use the technique, as do countless other people who have come to appreciate this way of reading and praying.

Four Ways to Read and Pray

Our object is to "open up" a scripture text by calling forth our ability to experience it in different modes. The Benedictine model suggests four activities: *lectio, meditatio, oratio,* and *contemplatio.* These Latin terms mean: read, meditate, pray, and contemplate. This four-mode pattern parallels Holmes's four spiritual types.

Lectio	READING	Uses SENSES to perceive	Kataphatic spirituality
Meditatio	MEDITATIO	Uses THINKING to reflect	Speculative spirituality
Oratio	PRAYER	Uses FEELING to respond	Affective spirituality
Contemplatio	CONTEMPLATION	Uses INTUITION to internalize	Apophatic spirituality

Those familiar with the Myers-Briggs Type Indicator test or the shorter Keirsey-Bates version may wonder if Jung's four basic psychological functions are also compatible with the *lectio divina* model. Yes, they are, as is evident from the third column, above. It probably is not advisable to force the Benedictine model into a parallel with Myers's multiple-letter categories, but the basic single-letter functions fit very well. For readers interested in adding to a spiritual direction library, I recommend *Prayer and Temperament: Different Prayer Forms for Different Personality Types*, by Michael and Norrisey.[1] Chapter 3 is a helpful comment on using *lectio divina* with the Jungian functions.

Preparation for *Lectio Divina*

Find a quiet, comfortable place and select a passage of scripture with which you want to work. You might be reading though the Psalms, using selections from the gospels or the Pentateuch, or you may be studying the assigned reading from a lectionary. A particular scripture may have come to mind as you considered concerns in your life, and you may want to follow up on that thought.

At first set aside at least thirty minutes. Eventually you will fall into a time-pattern that suits you. I have heard of people who set aside only fifteen minutes and others who spend well over an hour. Do what seems right for you at the time.

It is important, especially in our hurried culture, to do something to quiet the body before entering into this kind of interior reflection. Place your hand at your waist, close your eyes, and breathe down to your hand. This is a quick way of putting yourself in touch with your quieter, calmer self, and breaking away from the hectic pattern of clocks, telephone calls, memos, and lists. Once you become calm, you may be surprised to feel how much tension you have been carrying in your body, especially in the shoulders and jaw. For the moment, let the tensions and distractions go and enjoy the pleasant experience ahead of you.

In the next few pages I will explain the four activities suggested in the Benedictine model. These comments will be too long for you to read each time you want to pray a scripture passage in this way, so at the conclusion of the comments I give a short outline. Quickly refer to this short form as you use this method of reading and prayer. You have permission to make a copy of it to place in your Bible.

Group facilitators will find it easy to use *lectio divina* as a group activity. Have everyone read the same scripture passage, if discussion is to follow.

Briefly, the exercise involves reading instructions in the *"Lectio"* section below. Then read your selected scripture passage, thinking about the passage as the instructions suggest. Next read the *meditatio* instructions. Scan the scripture reading again, following the instructions. Then go on to *oratio* and *contemplatio*.

You may be delighted to discover a progression in your understanding—an unexpected unfolding of the scripture passage as you apply *all* your capabilities of perception. Typically, we engage only one or two. With this method all four functions are active, and each provides a dimension that adds depth to the whole. Let's break it down, now, into the four parts.

Lectio

As you begin, simply read the passage of scripture that you have selected in a careful, attentive way. Try not to think about the lessons you have gleaned in sermons or commentaries on this passage. This is not the time to think about what this piece *means*. That will come later. If you are responsible for teaching from this passage, put aside that concern for the moment. For now just get a sense of the atmosphere of the passage. If there is a setting involved, how is that described? Imagine the time of day, the season of the year, the smells and sounds of countryside or city. What events are taking place? Who are the characters involved? Use your imagination and senses to make the scene real to you. In other words, *be there*. If Isaiah is speaking, recall who he is and where he is. If Paul is writing, imagine the group or the person reading his letter and what you know of the Roman world of that time.

Those whose predominant spirituality type included the kataphatic (types 1 and 2) will especially enjoy the *lectio* section. It can engage your love for the concrete and the explainable. When a passage refers to God "speaking," you will have little difficulty hearing and seeing God in action. Fortunately for types 1 and 2, scripture is kataphatic in much of its presentation.

Meditatio

Here is the opportunity to *think* about what you have just sensed or ima-gined. Read the passage a second time asking, "What does this mean?" Why is there a record of this particular event or saying? What is the significance of this passage in the larger scheme of things? What does this passage mean to me personally? What is being demonstrated or shown? Ask the childlike "why?" If you have learned to think in theolo-gical categories, this is the time to bring to bear all that you know in un-derstanding the meaning of the passage. Ask yourself if a character in the scripture passage reminds you of yourself. Try to assume the role of all the characters in the story. That may help you get to the meaning of what is being said.

Types 1 and 4 enjoy this sort of inquiry. All types are able to ask and answer questions, but the type that includes the speculative function–the thinking type—does this the best.

Oratio

Now that you have imagined what is going on and have thought about the significance of all you have read, it is time to use your capacity to *feel emotion* as a way to open further the passage at hand. The first two activities, imagining and thinking, are very Western; we are trained to function in these ways. Fewer people can identify their feelings, so understanding the goal of this section may take some effort. Don't be intimidated if you are someone who typically shuts down your feelings. I think you can feel safe to experiment using this way of praying and reading.

Oratio means "speech," in this case speech to pray. As you begin to address God, or whatever you do as your way of praying, think also about how you now feel regarding this scripture. Review the passage a third time and name the feelings it raises within you. Finish the phrase: "I feel . . . " Is it anxious or confused? Perhaps you feel pity or love. Guilty, joyous, assured, or sad? Possibly you feel curious or even bored. There are no right or wrong feelings that go with this activity. Feelings just *are*, and if we try, we can usually name them. Silently or out loud, if that is how you pray best, talk about your feelings with God; tell God how you have responded to this passage of scripture. If you have had a feeling response that came to you from reading the passage, explain that to God as well as you can.

Types 2 and 3 will most enjoy this section. These two types share the affective or feeling function of the Spirituality Wheel. Type 2 may pray mostly with words, while type 3 may prefer to "feel" in God's presence. There are no rules as to how we pray, only that we communicate, which is what prayer fundamentally is.

Contemplatio

Apophatic spirituality involves contemplation, something we Westerners are not traditionally trained to do. To begin, most of us don't trust "that spooky stuff." Besides, we are virtually unable to sit quietly and have no object or thought in mind. I want to say a word to those who are fearful that learning the skills of contemplation is somehow promoting "another religion." It is true that Eastern religions do this better than most of us Westerners, but that does not mean they have an exclusive monopoly on the quiet, centering peacefulness that is available to any person who engages in contemplation. Actually, being contemplative can be a characteristic of people having no religious beliefs or practices. If we look into our own Judeo-Christian history, we find that there was quite a practice of and volume of writing about the contemplative life—most of it before the Industrial Revolution. It is demonstrably a part of our own heritage, a part that, to our harm, we have almost discarded.

In contemplation there is nothing to *do*. It is merely an attentive waiting or being present. If that sounds boring to you, give it time. As mentioned above, it is essential to quiet one's body, to feel relaxed and at ease. If you have not already done so, place your hand at your waist, close your eyes, and breathe down to your hand. Do this until your breathing is regular and natural. As you quiet your inner self, simply listen in your heart. If you have some impression or thought, quietly notice it; then return your attention to remaining open. If you have no thoughts or impressions, return your mind to the story or account you have just read. After a period of time that seems right to you, open your eyes, rested and refreshed, experiencing gratitude for the experience.

Contemplation is hard for Westerners because we want to know what to strive for while we are "doing it." It is difficult for us to expect nothing and to be satisfied with whatever happens or doesn't happen. In a word, we are goal-oriented. The goal of contemplation is quietly to listen and receive; even to receive silence. So what is the value? In this last and final stage of *lectio divina* one most often "owns" what has happened before; one internalizes what has taken place in the three previous activities. We are good at the first two, imagining and thinking, fair at the third, which is feeling, and often at a loss with the fourth, which has to do with really using our intuition. It is no wonder that scripture seems so unproductive and antiquated to many modern minds.

If you want some help with this fourth section, try asking a type 3. A type 4 can be adept at contemplation—if you can get her to put it on her schedule. Type 3 is the mystic, and these people often write the books and give the talks that furnish the rest of us with the inspiration and insight we so need to keep us going in our spiritual journey.

If you are leading a group in *lectio divina*, I suggest that you ask participants to read and go through the first three activities in silence. For the *contemplatio* section, you might ask group members to close their eyes, do the relaxation breathing, and then listen as you read aloud the instructions for this section. The less people have to do, such as reading, the more they can focus on what may be for them an unfamiliar experience.

(The Alban Institute grants permission for you to photocopy the following page.)

A Short Guide to *Lectio Divina*

Select a scripture passage.

Lectio: Read the passage carefully, getting the sequence and detail without thinking too much about the *meaning*. Imagine the time of day, season of the year, smells of the land, sounds of the countryside, the human touches—all the elements that would make this scene real to you. Transport yourself into the setting using your imagination.

Meditatio: Read the scripture again. Why is there a record of this particular event or saying? What is the significance of this passage in the larger scheme of things? What does this piece mean? How does that affect an understanding of God? Of conduct? Do you see yourself in any of the characters in the passage?

Oratio: Allow your feelings to surface as you read the passage again. Do you feel happy, sad, angry, or guilty? Silently or verbally talk this through with God; tell God what you feel about what you have read. Comment in your prayer on anything in the passage to which you respond.

Contemplatio: Sit quietly, breathe deeply and regularly, and let your mind go blank. As you quiet your inner self, simply listen in your heart. If you receive some impression or thought, quietly notice it; then focus your attention on remaining open. If you have no thoughts or impressions, return your mind to the scripture passage. After a while, open your eyes, rested and refreshed, expressing gratitude for your experience.

(From *Discover Your Spiritual Type: A Guide to Individual and Congregational Growth* by Corinne Ware, The Alban Institute, Inc. Copyright © 1995.)

CHAPTER IX

Spirituality and History

In his introduction to *A History of Christian Spirituality*, Urban T. Holmes made some brief observations about the relationship of styles of spirituality and the nature of human institutions. He makes it clear that his analysis is tentative—a theory. I find his propositions so interesting that the subject bears mentioning here. As we shall see, Holmes contends that a relationship exists between what is going on in history and what is being expressed spiritually within the culture.

Linking the Four Types to Historical Events

The following summary links historical circumstances to a pole of the Spirituality Wheel; when a particular circumstance is evident, says Holmes, a certain spirituality is called forth as a response.

- A sense of power and political predictability: speculative spirituality.
- Fewer boundaries and roles; less intellectual emphasis: affective spirituality.
- Sense of security: kataphatic spirituality.
- A collapse of social institutions: apophatic spirituality.

Holmes was a historian particularly interested in spiritual writings who inquired into the spiritual focus of various historical periods. He saw and identified distinctions among these periods.

Periods of Apophatic Expression

Holmes maintained, for instance, that prayer and devotional action of
the apophatic sort is an expression of the collapse of social institutions.
Apophatic expression, you remember, is the style of connecting that sees
God as mystery and as being unknowable. We say that those with an
affinity for this type of spirituality have a mystic tendency. Augustine
captured this spirituality in saying that we can know *that* God is, but we
cannot know *what* God is. There was an emphasis on this style during
the fourth and fifth centuries and again in the fourteenth century. The
fourth and fifth centuries were marked by political upheaval, including
the collapse of the Roman Empire. In the fourteenth century populations
were decimated by the Black Death, which killed a third of the residents
in many areas of Europe.

The twelfth and thirteenth centuries had been marked by a highly
speculative or intellectual spirituality. By the fourteenth century people
had become less intellectual; we see the decline of what was known as
scholasticism—the educational tradition of the medieval schools and the
philosophical inquiry that gave foundation to our own scientific method.
Scholasticism gave way to a particularly sterile philosophy called nominalism, which holds that we cannot really know anything about reality.
A corresponding spirituality emphasized intuition rather than deduction.

The fourteenth century was marked by a somber and pessimistic
mood. England and France were locked in a brutal and draining conflict,
the Hundred Years War, which was followed in England by the War of
the Roses. The Black Death, as noted above, swept western Europe. In
this stressful time, a group of religious known as the Rhineland Mystics
emerged producing John Tauler and Meister Eckhart, among others.
Eckhart believed that to know God, one must enter into "the darkness of
unknowing," certainly an apophatic approach. The spirituality of the
times emphasized a stripping away of the self, a mortification of the
flesh, and sometimes an anti-intellectualism that examined few of the
developing attitudes. A statement by Meister Eckhart is representative
of this period: "If you are to know God divinely, your own knowledge
must become as pure ignorance, in which you forget yourself and every
other creature."

Both spiritual insight and religious aberration came out of the
adversity of life in those times.

When people live with danger and stress, they turn to an other-worldly spirituality. Some call it escapism, and, if carried too far, it is. Remember the characteristic aberration of type 3, the apophatic-affective type, when it becomes overly focused on retreat and in denial of contextual reality? But if held in tension with a concrete, thinking function, the apophatic tendency can produce extraordinary spiritual insight. Just think about the mysticism evident in the Revelation of John, which concludes the New Testament. When persecution and adversity engulfed Spanish Jewry during the fifteenth century, the Kabbalistic interpretation of mystic spirituality helped the exiles to make sense of their suffering.

Periods of Affective Expression

Holmes points to the fifteenth century, following nominalism, as a period of pietism. If you remember, pietism is a type 2, affective-kataphatic spirituality carried to the extreme, not balanced by the tension exerted by the rest of the circle. Pietism typically follows a period of theological (speculative) sterility during which subjective feelings have been substituted for reason. Holmes also notes the pietism of the late seventeenth and eighteenth centuries, following Protestant scholasticism. More recently, a cultlike spirituality followed the "death of God" theology of the 1960s. Following such sterility of thought, the environment produces a rich imagery. There is a tendency by those looking for answers to dabble in the occult, particularly witchcraft, and what we are now calling "New Age." This dabbling is the pietism that is caused by over-reaction to sterile intellectualism. Evil is seen to be outside oneself, evidencing the perceived loss of personal power. Societal roles are not clearly defined, and the culture provides few moral anchors. A pietistic spirituality provides the wanted structure and externalizes danger so that it can be psychologically managed. Among the more insecure there is an almost frantic effort to somehow control what is out of control.

Periods of Speculative Expression

The antidote to this overly active affectivity (emotionalism) is a reasonable dose of the speculative. This sort of thinking spirituality occurs during times when there is relative political predictability and where the individual has a high sense of self-worth. Third-century Egypt and the twelfth-century Renaissance are examples, as well as the period of sixteenth-century humanism, and the eighteenth and nineteenth centuries in Europe. In these times "feeling" was balanced, even overtaken, by the cognitive function. The prevailing societal attitude was that life had promise; there was generally a dependable order to things. As we have seen, the ideal exists when there is an equal tension exerted between a speculative or thinking spirituality and an affective, or feeling, expression of religious experience.

Periods of Kataphatic Expression

Holmes does not cite a historical instance of the kataphatic spirituality, but within Christian history I would point to the security that came to the Christian church with the rule of Constantine. The creedal statement forged at the Council of Nicea in 325 and the later Calcedonian solution are about as concrete and incarnational as one can get.

Looking at Our Own Times

Anthropologist Mary Douglas suggests that when people have a low sense of personal power and when their roles are poorly defined, they have unclear internal boundaries and seek external certainties. Even evil itself is attributed to forces outside oneself, such as racial groups, political philosophies, the "government," or an ever-present Satan.[1] Certainly, in our own time we feel powerless and are confused about personal identity and our roles in society. We talk of "family values," hoping that our frequent references will bring back a more structured society. As has been pointed out, the antidote to the pietism we now experience is a thinking or speculative spirituality.

Modern Models

The solution to our modern malaise is not a return to overintellectualized spirituality. It is the balanced tensions of head and heart, of boundaries and freedom.

One who is able to hold these tensions creatively is the twentieth-century philosopher Martin Buber. Buber has a keen religious sensibility; his thinking is of the highest order, yet he feels deeply. His great gift is in making the secular sacred. "Buber taught me that mysticism need not lead outside the world," says his translator, Walter Kaufmann.[2] In fact, says Buber, experiences that lead one to forsake the world and its need are not of God but of the self and destructive. Buber is very clear about this union with the Thou, or the You, as never being otherworldly or detached. "I know nothing of 'worldly life' that separates us from God. . . . Whoever goes forth in truth to the world, goes forth to God."[3] He then talks of the necessary movement from plantlike security to the spiritual risk of encounter.

The only God worth keeping, says Buber, is the God who cannot be kept. God cannot be spoken of [in concrete terms], but God can be spoken to; God cannot be seen, but God can be listened to.

> For those who enter into the absolute relationship, nothing particular retains any importance—neither things nor beings, neither earth nor heaven—but everything is included in the relationship.[4]

That is to say, everything becomes sacred.

Buber combines all four spiritualities—thinking, feeling, imaging, and mystery; it is a model we can usefully explore in our day. He gives a profound insight that leads us to an "in the moment" feeling of relationship. For Buber the I-Thou relationship can exist only in the present moment; this existing second in time is the moment of intimacy, not the remembered past or the imagined future. Buber connects with the present reality as well as with the transcendent mystery. And the person who holds within him- or herself all the tensions in the circle offers us a model for healthy spirituality.

We might look also at the examples of others who had deep spiritual qualities yet who thoroughly engaged in secular life—people such as Dag Hammarskjöld and Simone Weil. Thomas Merton, himself a person who integrated the sacred and secular, describes such a tension.

> To be a person implies responsibility and freedom, and both these imply a certain interior solitude, a sense of personal

integrity, a sense of one's own reality and of one's ability to give himself to society.[5]

Present Trends

Observing present trends, we need only look at congregational demographics to discover that Americans are shifting their allegiances from speculative religion, which is often seen to be dry, mainline intellectualism, to the affective, or the "religion with heart." Much is gained by embracing a heart spirituality. Much is lost by abandoning the corrective of intellectual rigor that keeps a healthy tension on genuine warmth of feeling. *We must both feel and know.*

A second trend in our culture is the move toward the mystic, the transpersonal, and the transcendent. This is a good thing, generally speaking, and we certainly are in need of the corrective. The danger is that this quest, if unbalanced, can become enamored with magical beliefs based on little except the participant's wish that some object or ceremony will provide cheap power and total mind-body health. To abandon without serious consideration a tradition that has sustained us is to throw away a legacy that was hard-won. We may discover ourselves poorer for the loss.

We might easily wish for our times to be different so we could enjoy an ideal climate for spiritual and personal growth. Truly ideal times rarely come; if there are such moments, they occur as small pockets here and there.

Always and everywhere we are presented with circumstances and events we cannot entirely control. Yet our cultural climate is shaped by the attitudes of the people within it, and so it follows that each of us may become increasingly responsible for his or her own climate. Holmes's circle of spiritualities suggests the possibility of inclusiveness and of productive tension, encouraging the development of all parts of ourselves, as well as fostering within society the flowering of a healthy and balanced spirituality.

CHAPTER X

Fragmentation and Wholeness

In a society as diverse as ours, we look for commonalities that can bind us together. A group of Californians hope that speaking one language, English, will undo cultural fragmentation. Many Christian denominations participate in an established World Day of Prayer effort to assure themselves that they are united with Christendom in at least one action. Fearing more diversity, we turn away immigrants we once would have welcomed to our shores. When a national figure dies, television commentators note how we are suddenly "brought together" by our shock and grief. We notice gestures offering us hope that, for just a moment, we might be truly united as a people. Since we are becoming more, not less, diverse, and since society is as fragmented now as it has ever been, how do we achieve this common ground for which we yearn?

Formation for the Future

The subject of this book has been the study of a particular spirituality typology. The premise upon which these ideas of spiritual type rests assumes the benefit of both diversity and wholeness–of becoming individually ourselves while maintaining and appreciating a shared tradition. Both common tradition and individual uniqueness are valued and each is necessary to the general health.

We live with the knowledge that our cultural diversity is both curse and blessing. Managing that diversity in a productive way will require some changes in our thinking. Those shifts will involve seeing how our differences contribute to, more than they diminish, our quality of life. We will need to develop a tolerance for the "other."

A conceptual model for this wholeness is the circle divided by its intersecting lines. Although the lines cut the circle into individual parts, the parts remain together by being contained within the circle. Regarding the study of spiritual type, "there are many ways toward the vision, . . . the vision itself is one and exercises a control over the plurality of spiritual disciplines."[1]

The first of two requirements to any group becoming "one" is having a common vision. This is represented by the circle. The second requirement is the ability to allow differences while maintaining uniqueness. Using the spirituality types, this is demonstrated by the quadrants within the circle. Each brings a strength to the whole that enriches the whole. If I give up who I am, that does not help you. If I appreciate you, that helps us all. In religious practice, the common vision is that all creatures are connected to the Creator. Just how that connection to God is made is as various and individual as those who choose to seek it.

Global thoughts can be discouraging for those who want to make a difference for good in the world. The ideal of making us "one" is overwhelming, and, let's face it, it is not perfectly achievable. Several years ago a study was made of children with eating disorders. It was found that the children who would not eat enough at mealtime were being served plates loaded down with food. When the researchers offered the children plates holding only three small bites of food, the children regained their appetites. Just so, we become defeated by the overload of the world's adversity and its divisiveness; we feel overwhelmed and are paralyzed. Our "three bites of food" may be in seeing not the entire world but our smaller personal world as the field in which we can make a difference. Though challenging, it does seem more manageable.

The reader seeking to make a difference within his or her own world can consider the two audiences to whom this book is addressed: the individual whose spiritual journey and progress is of great personal importance, and the congregation and its leaders who want to better understand who they are spiritually. The Spirituality Wheel draws profiles of both.

As a result of what you learn about yourself and your worshipping congregation, you should see how well you both appreciate and use the gifts of others. You are not being asked to give up anything that is yours within your faith tradition (unless it is narrow exclusiveness). The idea of spiritual types suggests that differences are legitimate; that they reflect the God-made variety of created things. God is not threatened by what God has made nor should we be.

I trust there's a second result of your study of spiritual type: a new-found appreciation of your own spiritual nature. Chapter 1 opened with a short account of a woman whose story represents the concerns of many others. She was worried that she was "not religious enough" because her spiritual life was not like that of her friends. The message of the spiritual types is that the way we are is the way we need to be. We can grow, certainly, within that type, but we do not need to become other than we naturally are. Who we are is what is needed!

Possibilities for Wider Studies

As has been said previously, I developed the Spirituality Wheel Selector test as an effort to apply in a practical way the spirituality typology developed by Urban T. Holmes. The effort has accomplished what I hoped it would; it has given me a tool with which to help others discover their uniqueness and foster spiritual growth.

But I see potential for a wider application of the typology. Within a large faith group there will be a variety of congregations. A tension arises within the parent group: How much congregational diversity do we allow without losing institutional identity and witness? By testing the typology of the congregations within a faith group, leadership might gain insight as to whether the differences are those of spiritual expression based on differing types or if they are, indeed, doctrinal differences—a concern about belief, not style.

Another interesting inquiry would look into the spirituality type predominant among major faith groups. Are Presbyterians usually type-1 speculative-kataphatics, and are Eastern Orthodox Christians the only group with much representation in type 3? And what of the varieties within Jewish practice? Is the Reform branch essentially different in spirituality type from Orthodox Judaism? Which attracts whom?

The widest possible range of inquiry would be among the major religions of the world. Americans are now attracted by Eastern religions. Why is that? Is it because some with Western background are irresponsible and uninformed? Or is something missing in our contemporary Western religious expression? If so, should that missing thing be reclaimed, or would that be a betrayal of our faith history?

If a serious study of any of the suggested inquiries were to be undertaken, the first challenge would be to determine how Holmes's spirituality types could be translated into valid testing instruments for the purposes listed above. If these questions raise legitimate concerns for you, and if you are temperamentally suited to a study pursuit, this might make a valuable and fascinating project. For most people, the ideas presented here will make for interesting dialogue, at the very least. Readers with a keen grasp of the typology and of the groups to be considered might further discuss characteristics found in the comparison groups suggested here.

Remembering those children who were able to eat only when they saw small amounts on their plates, I challenge you to begin with yourself and with your local worshipping group. I also trust this study has told you something new about yourself—something that will prove valuable as you reach for growth. "Occasionally," says Lawrence Kushner, "a single word appears at the confluence of great intellectual currents. A word that seems to belong in each, yet combine all. In this generation, 'consciousness' is such a word."[2] What I have hoped for the reader is an increased consciousness of the whole and of its parts.

We become conscious of the fact that together we are like one body. It takes all the parts to make the whole, and each part is essential in some way to the health of the rest. It makes sense to be able to understand and to name which parts of the whole we are.

APPENDIX

Here are three slightly different versions of the statements used in the Spirituality Wheel Selector test, with a separate test page for each. The basic test, which also appears in chapter 4, is presented first. Its language and tone will be most familiar to Protestant Christian readers. Because of the differences in modes of worship and in vocabulary, somewhat altered versions have been prepared for the Roman Catholic reader and for the Jewish reader. It is essentially the same test. But the changes might describe experiences and feelings in more familiar language. Most Episcopalian readers will feel at home with the basic test, but those who belong to very formal, high-church congregations may prefer the Roman Catholic version of the test.

If you have further questions about how to take the test, review chapter 4.

The Spirituality Wheel©
Spirituality Type Selector Test
Basic Test

Corinne Ware, D. Min.

The purpose of this exercise is to DRAW A PICTURE of your experience of corporate worship and compare it to the picture of your own personal style of spirituality.

Before you start, look at the last page of the test. You will see two circles, each divided into quadrants numbered 1, 2, 3, and 4. Each quadrant stands for a type of spiritual expression. In the top circle, you will "draw a picture" of spiritual experience in your particular congregation. In the bottom circle, you will "draw a picture" of your personal style.

Congregational Style

Read through the first set of statements (starting below) and select the one(s) that describe what you do in your worshipping group. *You may select none or more than one if you wish.* Notice the number that goes with your chosen statement. On the *top* wheel on the last page of the test, find the numbered quadrant that matches the number of your chosen statement. In that quadrant draw a line (a spoke going from the center to the outside edge of the circle). If you've chosen two statements, draw two spokes, each in a different quadrant. Before you go on to the next set of statements, fill in the "personal style" wheel for the first set.

Personal Style

Read through the first set of statements a second time. Now choose the statement or statements that describe what you *personally* prefer as part of your spiritual experience. *You may select one statement or more than one.* Match the chosen statement number with the quadrant number in the lower circle. In that quadrant draw a spoke–line. If you've chosen two statements, draw two spokes, each in a different quadrant. The result is a portrait of your personal style, which you can compare with the experience you have in your worship group.

THE ORDER OF WORSHIP
1. A carefully planned and orderly worship program is a glory to God.
2. A deeply moving and spontaneous meeting is a glory to God.
3. Simplicity and some silence are important elements needed for worship.
4. It is not a service, but ordering ourselves to God's service that is important.

TIME
1. Stick to announced beginning and ending times of worship services.
2. It is important to extend the meeting time if one feels led to do so.
3. All time is God's time. A sense of timelessness is important.
4. Gather whenever and as long as you need to in order to accomplish the task.

PRAYER
1. Words express poetic praise; we ask for knowledge and guidance.
2. Let words and feelings evoke God's presence in this moment.
3. Empty the mind of distractions and simply BE in the presence of the Holy.
4. My life and my work are my prayer.

MUSIC
1. Music and lyrics express praise to God and belief about God.
2. Singing warms and unites us and expresses the soul's deepest heart.
3. Chant and tone bring the soul to quietness and union with God.
4. Songs can mobilize and inspire to greater effort and dedication.

PREACHING
1. The Word of God, rightly proclaimed, is the centerpiece of worship.
2. The gospel movingly preached is the power of God to change lives.
3. Proclamation is heard when the Spirit of God speaks to the inward heart.
4. What we do is our "preaching" and speaks louder than anything we say.

EMPHASIS
1. A central purpose is that we fulfill our vocation (calling) in the world.
2. A central purpose is that we learn to walk in holiness with the Lord.
3. A central purpose is that we be one with the Creator.
4. A central purpose is that we obey God's will completely.

SUPPORT OF CAUSES
(If necessary, circle the words that apply and select categories with the most circles.)
1. Support seminaries, publishing houses, scholarship, preaching to others.
2. Support evangelism, missions, spreading the word on television and radio.
3. Support places of retreat, spiritual direction, liturgical reform.
4. Support political action to establish justice in society and its institutions.

CRITICISM
1. Sometimes we (I) are said to be too intellectual, dogmatic, and "dry."
2. Sometimes we (I) are said to be too emotional, dogmatic, anti-intellectual.
3. Sometimes we (I) are said to be escaping from the world and are not realistic.
4. Sometimes we (I) are said to have tunnel vision and are too moralistic.

DOMINATING THEMES
(If necessary, circle the words that apply and select categories with the most circles.)
1. Discernment, discipline, knowledge, order, grace, justification.
2. Love, conversion, witness, spontaneity, sanctification.
3. Poverty, humility, wisdom, letting go, transcendence.
4. Simplicity, purity of heart, action, temperance, obedience, martyrdom.

MEMBERSHIP CRITERIA
(What the congregation believes is necessary; what you believe is necessary.)
1. Assent to doctrine; baptism; endorsement by group.
2. A personal inward experience of God; baptism; public declaration.
3. All who face Godward are incorporated in the Holy.
4. Solidarity with humankind is membership in God's kingdom.

RITUAL AND LITURGY
1. Ritual and liturgy evoke memory and presence, teaching traditional truths.
2. Liturgy and ritual ceremonies are not of great importance.
3. Ritual and liturgy are ways in which God becomes present to us.
4. Ritual and liturgy are one way we make statements about inner conviction.

CONCEPT OF GOD
1. God is revealed in scripture, sacrament, and in Jesus Christ and his cross.
2. I can feel that God is real and that Christ lives in my heart.
3. God is mystery and can be grasped for but not completely known.
4. We participate in the mystery of God when we become co–creators with God in the world.

The Spirituality Wheel©
A Selector for Spiritual Type
Corinne D. Ware, D. Min.
Based on a spirituality typology developed by Urban T. Holmes

CONGREGATIONAL STYLE

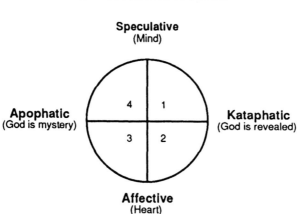

PERSONAL STYLE

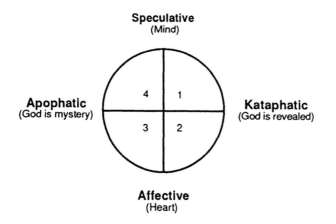

Adapted from *The History of Christian Spirituality: An Analytical Introduction* by Urban T. Holmes, © The Seabury Press. Used by permission of Jane Holmes, Executrix.

The Spirituality Wheel©
Spirituality Type Selector Test
Catholic Version

Corinne Ware, D. Min.

The purpose of this exercise is to DRAW A PICTURE of your experience of corporate worship and compare it to the picture of your own personal style of spirituality.

Before you start, look at the last page of the test. You will see two circles, each divided into quadrants numbered 1, 2, 3, and 4. Each quadrant stands for a type of spiritual expression. In the top circle, you will "draw a picture" of spiritual experience in your particular congregation. In the bottom circle, you will "draw a picture" of your personal style.

Congregational Style

Read through the first set of statements (starting below) and select the one(s) that describe what you do in your worshipping group. *You may select none or more than one if you wish.* Notice the number that goes with your chosen statement. On the *top* wheel on the last page of the test, find the numbered quadrant that matches the number of your chosen statement. In that quadrant draw a line (a spoke going from the center to the outside edge of the circle). If you've chosen two statements, draw two spokes, each in a different quadrant. Before you go on to the next set of statements, fill in the "personal style" wheel for the first set.

Personal Style

Read through the first set of statements a second time. Now choose the statement or statements that describe what you *personally* prefer as part of your spiritual experience. *You may select one statement or more than one.* Match the chosen statement number with the quadrant number in the lower circle. In that quadrant draw a spoke–line. If you've chosen two statements, draw two spokes, each in a different quadrant. The result is a portrait of your personal style, which you can compare with the experience you have in your worship group.

THE ORDER OF WORSHIP
1. A carefully ordered worship service is a glory to God.
2. A deeply moving service is a glory to God.
3. Simplicity and some silence are the things most needed.
4. It is not the service of liturgy, but serving God in others that is important.

TIME
1. Stick to announced beginning and ending times of services.
2. It is important to be as flexible as possible, letting The Spirit lead.
3. All time is God's time. A sense of timelessness is important.
4. Gather whenever and as long as you need to in order to accomplish the task.

PRAYER
1. Words express poetic praise; we ask for knowledge and guidance.
2. Let words and feelings evoke God's presence in this moment.
3. Empty the mind of distractions and simply BE in the presence of the Holy.
4. My life and my work are my prayer.

MUSIC
1. Music and words express praise to God and belief about God.
2. Singing unites us, and expresses the soul's deepest heart.
3. Chant and tone bring the soul to quietness and union with God.
4. Songs can mobilize and inspire to greater effort and dedication.

PREACHING
1. The Word of God, rightly proclaimed, is an important part of worship.
2. The scripture movingly preached is the power of God to change lives.
3. Proclamation is heard when the Spirit of God speaks to the inward heart.
4. What we do is our "preaching," and speaks louder than anything we say.

RELIGIOUS EMPHASIS
1. A central purpose is that we fulfill our vocation in the world.
2. A central purpose is that we learn to walk in holiness with the Lord.
3. A central purpose is that we be united with the Creator.
4. A central purpose is that we obey God's will completely.

INTEREST IN CAUSES
(If necessary, circle the words that apply and select categories with the most circles.)
1. Support seminaries, publishing houses, scholarship, preaching.
2. Support of evangelism, missions, spreading the word on television and radio
3. Support places of retreat, spiritual direction, liturgical reform.
4. Support political action to establish justice in society and its institutions.

CRITICISM
1. Sometimes we (I) are said to be too intellectual, dogmatic, and formal.
2. Sometimes we (I) are said to be too emotional, dogmatic, and uncritical.
3. Sometimes we (I) are said to be escaping from the world and not realistic.
4. Sometimes we (I) are said to be too moralistic and crusading.

DOMINATING THEMES
(If necessary, circle the words that apply and select categories with the most circles.)
1. Discernment, discipline, knowledge, order, grace, justification.
2. Love, conversion, witness, spontaneity, sanctification.
3. Poverty, wisdom, humility, letting go, transcendence.
4. Simplicity, purity of heart, action, temperance, obedience, martyrdom.

MEMBERSHIP CRITERIA
(What the congregation believes is necessary; what you believe is necessary.)
1. Assent to doctrine; baptism; endorsement by the group.
2. A personal experience of God; baptism; and showing our joy.
3. All who face Godward are incorporated in the Holy.
4. Solidarity with humankind is membership in God's kingdom.

RITUAL AND LITURGY
1. Ritual and liturgy evoke memory and presence, teaching traditional truths.
2. Liturgy and ritual ceremonies are not as important as some think.
3. Ritual and liturgy are ways in which God becomes present to us.
4. Ritual and liturgy are ways we make statements about our inner conviction.

CONCEPT OF GOD
1. God is revealed in scripture, sacrament, and in Jesus Christ and his cross.
2. I can feel that God is real and that Christ lives in my heart.
3. God is mystery and can be grasped for but not completely known.
4. We participate in the mystery of God when we become co-creators with God in the world.

The Spirituality Wheel©
A Selector for Spiritual Type

Corinne D. Ware, D. Min.
Based on a spirituality typology developed by Urban T. Holmes

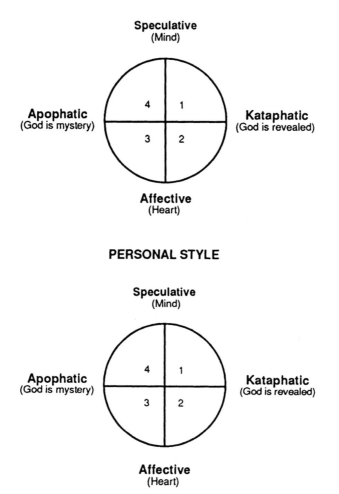

CONGREGATIONAL STYLE

Speculative
(Mind)

Apophatic
(God is mystery)

Kataphatic
(God is revealed)

Affective
(Heart)

PERSONAL STYLE

Speculative
(Mind)

Apophatic
(God is mystery)

Kataphatic
(God is revealed)

Affective
(Heart)

Adapted from *The History of Christian Spirituality: An Analytical Introduction* by Urban T. Holmes, © The Seabury Press. Used by permission of Jane Holmes, Executrix.

The Spirituality Wheel©
Spirituality Type Selector Test
Jewish Version

Corinne Ware, D. Min.

The purpose of this exercise is to DRAW A PICTURE of your experience of corporate worship and compare it to the picture of your own personal style of spirituality.

Before you start, look at the last page of the test. You will see two circles, each divided into quadrants numbered 1, 2, 3, and 4. Each quadrant stands for a type of spiritual expression. In the top circle, you will "draw a picture" of spiritual experience in your particular congregation. In the bottom circle, you will "draw a picture" of your personal style.

Congregational Style

Read through the first set of statements (starting below) and select the one(s) that describe what you do in your worshipping group. *You may select none or more than one if you wish.* Notice the number that goes with your chosen statement. On the *top* wheel on the last page of the test, find the numbered quadrant that matches the number of your chosen statement. In that quadrant draw a line (a spoke going from the center to the outside edge of the circle). If you've chosen two statements, draw two spokes, each in a different quadrant. Before you go on to the next set of statements, fill in the "personal style" wheel for the first set.

Personal Style

Read through the first set of statements a second time. Now choose the statement or statements that describe what you *personally* prefer as part of your spiritual experience. *You may select one statement or more than one.* Match the chosen statement number with the quadrant number in the lower circle. In that quadrant draw a spoke–line. If you've chosen two statements, draw two spokes, each in a different quadrant. The result is a portrait of your personal style, which you can compare with the experience you have in your worship group.

THE ORDER OF WORSHIP
1. A carefully planned and orderly worship service is a glory to God.
2. A deeply moving and spontaneous worship service is a glory to God.
3. Simplicity and some silence are the most important elements needed.
4. It is not a service, but ordering ourselves *to* God's service that is important.

TIME
1. Stick to announced beginning and ending times of worship services.
2. It is important to extend the meeting time if one feels moved to do so.
3. All time is God's time. A sense of timelessness is important.
4. Gather whenever and as long as you need to in order to accomplish the task.

PRAYER
1. Words express poetic praise; we ask for knowledge and guidance.
2. Let words and feelings evoke God's presence in this moment.
3. Empty the mind of distractions and simply BE in the presence of the Holy.
4. My life and my work are my prayer.

MUSIC
1. Music and words express praise to God and belief about God.
2. Singing warms and unites us, and expresses the soul's deepest heart.
3. Traditional singing can bring the soul to quietness and union with God.
4. Songs can mobilize and unite to greater effort and dedication.

PREACHING
1. The hearing and study of scripture is the centerpiece of worship.
2. The sermon movingly preached is the power of God to change lives.
3. The Word of God is heard when the Spirit of God speaks to the inward heart.
4. What we do is our "preaching," and speaks louder than anything we say.

RELIGIOUS EMPHASIS
1. A central purpose is that we fulfill our destiny in the world.
2. A central purpose is that we learn to walk in holiness with the Lord.
3. A central purpose is that we be united with the Creator.
4. A central purpose is that we keep the Law as completely as possible.

SUPPORT OF CAUSES
(If necessary, circle the words that apply and select categories with the most circles.)
1. Support seminaries, publishing houses, scholarship, preaching.
2. Support telling our story to others in person, on television, and radio.
3. Support places of retreat, spiritual studies, liturgical reform.
4. Support political action to establish justice in society and its institutions.

CRITICISM
1. Sometimes we (I) are said to be too intellectual, dogmatic, and "dry."
2. Sometimes we (I) are said to be too emotional, dogmatic, and illogical.
3. Sometimes we (I) are said to be escaping from the world and not realistic.
4. Sometimes we are said to have tunnel vision, and are too moralistic and intense.

DOMINATING THEMES
(If necessary, circle the words that apply and select categories with the most circles.)
1. Discipline, knowledge, order, tradition.
2. Love, conversion, witness, spontaneity.
3. Wisdom, humility, letting go, transcendence.
4. Simplicity, purity of heart, action, temperance, obedience, martyrdom.

MEMBERSHIP CRITERIA
(What the congregation believes is necessary; what you believe is necessary.)
1. Assent to certain beliefs and/or acceptance by the group.
2. A personal experience of God; making this known to others.
3. All who face Godward are incorporated in the Holy.
4. Solidarity with humankind is membership in God's kingdom.

RITUAL
1. Ritual evokes memory and presence, teaching traditional truths.
2. Ritual ceremonies are not as important as some think.
3. Ritual is a way in which God becomes present to us.
4. Ritual is one way we make statements about our beliefs and identity.

CONCEPT OF GOD
1. God is revealed in Torah, ritual, and tradition.
2. I can feel that God lives in my heart.
3. God is mystery and can be grasped for but not completely known.
4. We participate in the mystery of God when we become co-creators with God in the world.

The Spirituality Wheel©
A Selector for Spiritual Type

Corinne D. Ware, D. Min.
Based on a spirituality typology developed by Urban T. Holmes

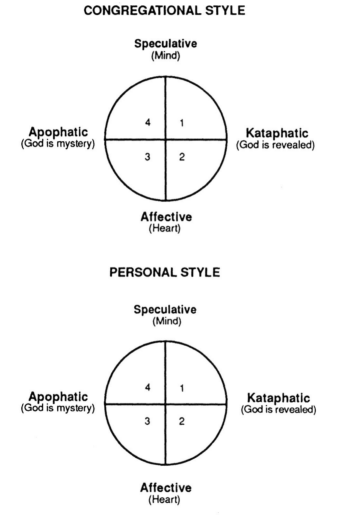

CONGREGATIONAL STYLE

Speculative
(Mind)

Apophatic
(God is mystery)

Kataphatic
(God is revealed)

Affective
(Heart)

PERSONAL STYLE

Speculative
(Mind)

Apophatic
(God is mystery)

Kataphatic
(God is revealed)

Affective
(Heart)

Adapted from *The History of Christian Spirituality: An Analytical Introduction* by Urban T. Holmes, © The Seabury Press. Used by permission of Jane Holmes, Executrix.

NOTES

Chapter 1

1. Carl G. Jung, *Psychological Types*, tran. R. R. C. Hull, ed.
William McGuire, Collected Works 6, Bollingen Series XX (Princeton,
N.J.: Princeton University Press, 1921).
2. Isabel Briggs Myers, *The Myers-Briggs Type Indicator* (Palo Alto,
Calif.: Consulting Psychologists Press, 1962).
3. David Kiersey and Marilyn Bates, *Please Understand Me: An
Essay on Temperament Styles* (Del Mar, Calif.: Prometheus Nemesis
Books, 1978).
4. Urban T. Holmes, A History of Christian Spirituality: An Analytical Introduction (Minneapolis: Seabury, 1980), 3-7.
5. Ibid., 5.

Chapter 2

1. M. Scott Peck, M.D., from a speech made to the American Psychiatric Association, May 1992, quoted by Michael J. McManus, "Ethics
and Religion," in *St. Joseph News-Press,* 1 August 1992, 3.
2. Robert Jean Campbell, M.D., *Psychiatric Dictionary*, 6th ed.
(New York: Oxford University Press, 1987), 377.
3. Abraham H. Maslow, *Religions, Values, and Peak-Experiences*
(New York: Penguin, 1964), vii.
4. Leo Booth, *When God Becomes a Drug: Breaking the Chains of
Religious Addiction and Abuse* (New York: J. P. Tarcher, 1991).

5. Robert J. Lovinger, *Working With Religious Issues in Therapy* (New York: Jason Aronson, 1984).

6. C. G. Jung, *Psychological Types*, trans. R. R. C. Hull, ed. William McGuire, Collected Works 6, Bollingen Series XX (Princeton, N.J.: Princeton University Press, 1921), pars. 1-7.

7. Margaret S. Mahler, "On the Current Status of the Infantile Neurosis," *The Selected Papers of Margaret S. Mahler, M.D.*, vol. 2 (New York: Jason Aronson, 1975), 187-93.

8. Gershen Kaufman, *Shame: The Power of Caring*, 2nd ed., rev. (Rochester, Vt.: Schenkman Books, 1980), 135.

9. Urban T. Holmes, *A History of Christian Spirituality: An Analytical Introduction* (Minneapolis: Seabury, 1980), 4. Holmes uses the word *Christian* here. I have inserted the bracketed word *religious* because of the present application to faiths other than Christian.

10. Martin Buber, *I and Thou*, trans. Walter Kaufmann (New York: Scribners, 1970), 116.

11. Marcus J. Borg, *Jesus: A New Vision* (San Francisco: Harper & Row, 1987), 9.

12. E. P. Sanders, *Jesus and Judaism* (Philadelphia: Fortress, 1985), 326.

13. Abraham Heschel, *The Prophets*, vol. 1 (New York: Harper & Row, 1962), 22.

14. Matthew Fox, "Meister Eckhart on the Fourfold Path of a Creation-Centered Spiritual Journey," in *Western Spirituality: Historical Roots, Ecumenical Routes*, ed. Matthew Fox (Santa Fe, N.M.: Bear, 1981), 234.

15. Gershom Scholem, *Major Trends in Jewish Mysticism* (New York: Schocken, 1946), iii.

16. Aryeh Kaplan, *Jewish Meditation: A Practical Guide* (New York: Schocken, 1985), 3.

17. J. C. Rylaarsdam, *Revelation in Jewish Wisdom Literature* (Chicago: University of Chicago Press, 1946), 55.

18. John H. Hayes, *An Introduction to Old Testament Study* (Nashville: Abingdon, 1979), 337.

19. Harvey Cox, "Rabbi Yeshua ben Joseph," *The Pennsylvania Gazette* 87 (December 1988): 17.

20. C. H. Dodd, *The Parables of the Kingdom* (New York: Scribners, 1961), 5.

21. M. D. Chenu, "Body and Body Politic in the Creation Spirituality of Thomas Aquinas," in *Western Spirituality: Historical Roots, Ecumenical Routes*, ed. Matthew Fox (Sante Fe, N.M.: Bear, 1981), 204.

22. Stanley Hauerwas and William Willimon, "Embarrassed by God's Presence," *Christian Century* 102 (January 30, 1985): 98-100.

23. Thomas Moore, *Care of the Soul: A Guide for Cultivating Depth and Sacredness in Everyday Life* (New York: Harper Collins, 1992), 11.

24. Rudolf Otto, *The Idea of the Holy* (New York: Oxford University Press, 1958), 156.

25. *The R.S.V. Interlinear Greek–English New Testament* (Grand Rapids: Zondervan, 1988).

26. Heschel, *The Prophets*, 224.

27. Geza Vermes, *Jesus the Jew* (New York: Macmillan, 1973), 224.

28. Howard Clinebell, *Growth Counseling: Hope-Centered Methods of Actualizing Human Wholeness* (Nashville: Abingdon, 1979), 108.

Chapter 3

1. Joan Rachel Goldberg, "Spirituality, Religion and Secular Values: What Role in Psychotherapy?" *Family Therapy News* (June 1994): 9.

2. Isabel Briggs Myers, *The Myers-Briggs Type Indicator* (Palo Alto, Calif.: Consulting Psychologists Press, 1962).

3. W. Paul Jones, "Myers-Briggs Type Indicator: A Psychological Tool for Approaching Theology and Spirituality," *Weavings* 6 (1991): 32-43.

4. W. Paul Jones to author, November 27, 1991.

5. Robert E. Ornstein, *The Psychology of Consciousness* (New York: Penguin, 1972), 12.

6. Arthur J. Deikman, "Bimodal Consciousness," *Archives of General Psychiatry* 25 (December 1971): 481-89.

7. Arthur J. Deikman, "Deautomatization and the Mystic Experience," *Psychiatry* 29 (1966): 324-38.

8. Victor Turner, *The Ritual Process: Structure and Anti-Structure* (Ithaca, N.Y.: Cornell University Press, 1969).

9. John of the Cross, *Dark Night of the Soul*, trans. E. Allison Peers (Garden City, N.Y.: Doubleday, Image, 1959), 91.

10. Urban T. Holmes, *The Priest in Community: Exploring the Roots of Ministry* (New York: Seabury, 1978), 95.

11. Ibid., 146.

12. Abraham Maslow, quoted by Robert E. Ornstein, ed., *The Nature of Human Consciousness: A Book of Readings* (New York: Viking, 1973), 3.

13. Lawrence LeShan and Henry Margenau, *Einstein's Space and Van Gogh's Sky* (New York: Macmillan, 1982), xii.

14. Allan H. Sager, *Gospel-Centered Spirituality: An Introduction to Our Spiritual Journey* (Minneapolis: Augsburg, 1990), 38. See chapter 2 for a discussion of Holmes's four spiritual types, for Sager's forced-choice test, and for an excellent graphic of the circle (p. 36).

15. Wade Clark Roof and William McKinney, *American Mainline Religion: Its Changing Shape and Future* (New Brunswick, N.J.: Rutgers University Press, 1987), 171, 172.

16. Sager, *Gospel-Centered Spirituality*, 47.

17. Anthony de Mello, *Sadhana, a Way to God: Christian Exercises in Eastern Form* (Garden City, N.Y.: Doubleday, Image, 1984). (One example among several of de Mello's books.)

18. Thomas Merton, *No Man Is an Island* (San Diego: Harcourt Brace Jovanovich, 1955). (One example among several of Merton's books.)

19. Gershom Scholem, *On the Kabbalah and Its Symbolism*, trans. Ralph Manheim (New York: Schocken, 1965). (One among several of Scholem's writings on Jewish mysticism.)

20. Lawrence Kushner, *Honey from the Rock: Visions of Jewish Mystical Renewal* (New York: Harper & Row, 1977). (One example among several of Kushner's books.)

21. Matthew Fox, *Original Blessing: A Primer on Creation Spirituality* (Santa Fe, N.M.: Bear, 1983). (One example of this genre.)

Chapter 6

1. Stephen Ministries trains laypeople for church ministry: visiting skills; pastoral care of the grieved, depressed, ill, dying, elderly, and housebound; also for those facing divorce and family crisis, among other problematic situations. Stephen Ministries, 8016 Dale Ave., St. Louis, MO 63117; (314) 645-5511.

Chapter 7

1. Isabel Briggs Myers, *Gifts Differing* (Palo Alto, Calif.: Consulting Psychologists Press, 1980).

Chapter 8

1. Chester P. Michael and Marie C. Norrisey, *Prayer and Temperament: Different Prayer Forms for Different Personality Types* (Charlottesville, Va.: Open Door, 1984).

Chapter 9

1. Mary Douglas, as quoted in Urban T. Holmes, *The History of Christian Spirituality: An Analytical Introduction* (Minneapolis: Seabury, 1980), 9.

2. Walter Kaufmann, "Preface," in Martin Buber, *I and Thou,* trans. Walter Kaufmann (New York: Scribners, 1970).

3. Martin Buber, *I and Thou,* trans. Walter Kaufmann (New York: Scribners, 1970), 143.

4. Ibid., 127.

5. Thomas Merton, *Thoughts in Solitude* (New York: Farrar, Straus & Giroux, 1981), 13.

Chapter 10

1. John Macquarrie, *Principles of Christian Theology*, 2nd ed. (New York: Scribners, 1977), 499.

2. Lawrence Kushner, *The River of Light* (Woodstock, Vt.: Jewish Lights, 1981), xv.

(These quotations are also printed in the epigraph.)

① Abraham Maslow
② The Imitation of Christ
        Thomas à Kempis

Printed in the United States
201740BV00005B/193-315/P